Celebrations of Faith

Celebrations of Faith

tying our children's heartstrings to the truth

Randy&Lisa
Wilson
with Beth Lueders

Creating Teachable Moments
faithparenting.com

Faith Parenting is an imprint of
Cook Communications Ministries, Colorado Springs, Colorado 80918
Cook Communications, Paris, Ontario
Kingsway Communications, Eastbourne, England

CELEBRATIONS OF FAITH
© 2001 by Randy and Lisa Wilson

First Printing, 2001
Printed in the United States of America

1 2 3 4 5 6 7 8 9 10 Printing/Year 05 04 03 02 01

Cover Design: Alan Furst
Interior Design: Image Studios

Unless otherwise noted, Scripture quotations are taken from the *Holy Bible: New
International Version*®. Copyright © 1973, 1978, 1984 by International Bible Society.
Used by permission of Zondervan Publishing House. All rights reserved.
Additional Scripture quotations are taken from *New American Standard Bible* (NASB),
© the Lockman Foundation 1960, 1962, 1963, 1968, 1971, 1972, 1973, 1975,
1977; *The New King James Version* (NKJV). © 1979, 1980, 1982, Thomas Nelson,
Inc., Publishers; *King James Version* (KJV).

Library of Congress Cataloging-in-Publication Data

Wilson, Randy (David Randall)
    Celebrations of Faith : tying your children's heartstrings to God's truth /
Randy and Lisa Wilson, with Beth Lueders.
        p. cm.
    ISBN 0-7814-3508-0
    1. Family--Religious life. I. Wilson, Lisa. II. Lueders, Beth. III. Title.

    BV4526.2 .W555 2001
    249--dc21

                                                                00-062263

Acknowledgments

To our parents, who've modeled faithfulness and love to us, who've blessed, encouraged, and believed in us, always. We love you and gratefully honor you!

To our mentors, who've walked with us through various seasons of our lives, encouraging, directing, praying, laughing, and crying with us and never giving up on us!

Bruce and Bev – you've encouraged and loved us for 20 years patiently walking with us as we stumbled through growing pains of dating, engagement, marriage, ministry, and each of our babies. You've been so faithful. We love you dearly. You are holy examples of a loving God to us.

Pat and Annie, your transparence and vulnerability in your walk of faith showed us more of God than you'll ever know. Your gentle, trusting clinging to God encouraged us to trust Him in our dark times.

Sonny and Judy, your openness in mentoring us with all our questions on family was a beacon of light and beauty. Thank you for letting us watch and learn from you.

Jack and Bev, you've relentlessly prayed for us all these years, encouraged us to persevere, listened to our struggles in seeking God, and loved us unconditionally.

Dick and Kay, your godly lives and wise counsel have shown us the heart of God. Your authenticity is refreshing. You have fanned the flame of God's vision for us. Thank you for walking with us.

Paul and Phyllis, your love of the Truth and commitment to live it and teach it has ministered to our family for years. Your direction, advice, and support have led us to this place. Thank you for always seeing the best and loving us.

And of course, we honor our 6 children with this book. Each celebration started quietly in our little home, in our desire to pour God into these 6 hearts. You are our joy, crown, and glory! We love you deeply, Lauren, Colten, Khrystian, Jordan, Logan, and Kameryn!

Thank you, Derek and Lee, at Cook, for catching our vision and the incredible job you've done making this happen!

Contents

PART ONE: A Reason to Celebrate

PART TWO: The Gift of Perspective

PART ONE

A Reason to Celebrate

1
Our Children's Heartbeats

> **"The things that matter most must never be at the mercy of things that matter least."**
> —*Goethe* [1]

Scribbling notes to himself, the young doctor snapped out a series of clipped questions: "Any fever?" . . . "Any signs of fatigue?" . . . "How's his appetite?"

As we answered the brusque inquiries by our pediatrician's associate, our four-year-old Logan curiously scanned the examining room with his bright blue eyes. We had quickly scheduled this check-up because Randy had noticed a slight irregularity in Logan's heartbeat.

Moving matter-of-factly through his checklist of questions, the doctor finally paused and turned to Randy. "Well, how do you *know* that his heartbeat is different? Maybe it's been like this since birth and you haven't noticed it."

"I know the heartbeats of my children," Randy calmly replied in measured words, looking the physician in the eyes. "Every night when I put my children down and pray with them, I lay my head on their chests, and I hear their heartbeats. The heartbeat Logan had on Saturday night was not the same heartbeat he had on Sunday night."

The young doctor's face froze in bewilderment. He sat speechless at Randy's summary of our son's health. Staring silently at his clipboard for several seconds, the dumbfounded doctor finally answered, "Really?"

The doctor then attributed Logan's murmur to a possible virus and advised us to monitor him carefully for a few days. Fortunately Logan showed no further signs of a murmur. While the doctor assessed the heartbeat of our son, God was pleased with the heart of a father.

This young doctor may have labeled us an "unusual case," but it's true that over the years we've learned to recognize the physical, emotional, and spiritual heartbeats of each of our six children. We know, as one old farmer used to say, "what makes them tick."

The only way we can know the heartbeats of our children is to be consistently present and intimately involved in their lives. This book is about listening to the deeper sounds of the hearts and souls of our children and finding creative ways to tie their heartstrings to God's truth.

Throughout our sixteen years of parenting, God has given us a number of ideas that we call *Celebrations of Faith*—ceremonies and events that reflect the goodness of God and remind our children to look back and see Him at work in their lives. You'll soon discover how to adopt some of these fun and memorable practices for your own family.

following God's lead

We are grateful that the Lord set aside God-fearing relatives in our lineage who carried the torch of His Word. Both of us, by God's grace, placed our faith in Christ before we were seven years old. When we were married in 1982, neither of us had any idea where life's road would take us, but God did.

When Lisa was pregnant with our first child, we began to ponder the incredible responsibility and privilege of raising a generation who would know and love their God. As we looked at our family heritage and the faith passed down to us, we knew that God had chosen us to impart our love for Him to the next generation.

As a newly married couple, we saw God's hand on us when our start-up construction company in Austin, Texas, nose-dived along with the local oil and real estate market. We lost everything and had to begin again. In the midst of the stress and uncertainty, godly mentors directed us to Isaiah 50:10-11:

> Who among you fears the LORD and obeys the word of his servant? Let him who walks in the dark, who has no light, trust in the name of the LORD and rely on his God. But now, all you who light fires and provide yourselves with flaming torches, go, walk in the light of your fires and of the torches you have set ablaze. This is what you shall receive from my hand: You will lie down in torment.

In our dark times, we knew we needed to "trust in the name of the LORD" and not light our own torches to see our way through. God used this unsettling experience to bolster our faith and remind us to rely on Him and "dwell in the land and cultivate faithfulness" (Ps. 37:3, NASB).

Waiting for God's light to pierce our darkness is like the marvelous process of creating lace. In Brussels, which produces exquisite lace, famous shops devote special rooms to spinning delicate lace patterns. Each room is completely darkened, except for a glimmer of light from one tiny window. A spinner sits in the one spot where the outside light shines on the threads of his weaving. *The most gorgeous lace is woven when the worker stays in the dark and his pattern remains in the light.*[2]

In our days clouded with unknowns, we learned to embrace the gift of darkness that God uses to weave His marvelous pattern for our lives. We learned to focus on even a glimmer of God's light.

Whether you are parenting with your spouse or parenting solo, God wants you to dwell, or settle, in your circumstances. He wants to empower you with faithfulness. He promises to be the lamp to your feet and light to your path (Ps. 119:105), especially when you're tempted to light your own torches. The Light of the World stands ready to be your daily guide in your tremendous role as parent.

passing on His flame

Right now, you may feel as though your flame as a parent is barely alive. But the Lord reassures us in Isaiah 42:3, "A bruised reed He will not break, and a dimly burning wick He will not extinguish" (NASB). As you read this book, you may think, *I'm overwhelmed and feel inadequate to try even one of these celebrations with my kids.* Yet, as we've experienced time and time again, God Almighty will breathe into you the passion that you need to do His work. God will generously pour out His grace on you as you determine to pass on His divine truths to future generations.

You may not come from a legacy of people of faith, but God knows that. Regardless of your family background or your present challenges as a parent, God wants to use you to pass a baton of spiritual faithfulness to your children, their children, and their children's children. "For you know that it was not with perishable things such as silver or gold that you were redeemed from the empty way of life handed down to you from your forefathers, but with the precious blood of Christ, a lamb without blemish or defect" (1 Peter 1:18-19). It all starts with you!

Abraham, the patriarch of Israel, descended from a family that worshiped idols. He lacked a righteous background. Yet God said, "You're mine, and you're going this way." God chose Abraham and placed him on a special path. He became God's man to lead His people. God will do the same for you. You are on a God-directed journey of nurturing each child God has entrusted to you.

You are called to be His light and pass on His flame to your children. But, thankfully, you are not alone. Thousands of parents like us are running alongside you. As mothers and fathers, we have the privilege to partner with a holy God to usher in His kingdom to the next generation.

investing in tomorrow today

Throughout Scripture, God discusses the importance of today's fathers and mothers influencing tomorrow's fathers and mothers. Psalm 112:1-2 proclaims, "Praise the LORD! How blessed is the man who fears the LORD, who greatly delights in His commandments. His descendants will be mighty on earth; the generation of the upright will be blessed" (NASB).

When we surrender our lives to God and delight in His commands, He promises to extend rich blessings to our family for years to come. Even before our children are born, He has ordained for them to tell their own children of the wonders of His love:

> He commanded our fathers, that they should teach them to their children, that the generation to come might know, even the children yet to be born, that they may arise and tell them to their children, that they should put their confidence in God, and not forget the works of God, but keep His commandments (Ps. 78:5-7, NASB).

Even from the *womb*, God sets us apart! He shows us in Scripture how even babies take part in spiritual matters. Luke 1:15 declares of John the Baptist: "he will be filled with the Holy Spirit even from birth." And 2 Timothy 3:15 states, "from infancy you have known the holy Scriptures."

When noted architect Frank Lloyd Wright was still in his mother's womb, she would pace in front of large, elegant pictures of architecture and describe these masterpieces to her unborn son. What impact are you leaving on your children even from their days in the womb and from their infancy?

In one of her inspiring messages, Elisabeth Elliot has said, "The very presence of a redeemed family has an incalculable impact on our fallen world." How is your family making an impact on our world? How are you investing your time for all eternity?

minutes versus moments

The Bible talks about time in two ways. *Chronos* is the years, days, hours, and the *minutes* of our lives. This includes the details of our schedules and appointments. In the New Testament, *chronos* or "measured time" is listed fifty-four times.

Kairos, which is mentioned eighty-five times in the New Testament, refers to the *moments* of our lives when time seems to stand still. *Kairos* moments are the memories, the special celebrations in our lives. These include unforgettable moments that change the direction of our lives—celebrating our wedding, holding our newborn for the first time, teaching our child to ride a bike.

Minutes become moments when God's kingdom time enters into earthly time. It's the everyday moments that shape our character and our lives. The power of a legacy is passed down in remembering these moments. "Remember" in the Hebrew means "incense," or literally "a fragrance to God's heart." We love this!

The power of our memory is a God-given gift. Brenda Hunter in her book *Home by Choice* tells the story of Wilder Penfield's research on the human brain. Penfield used a microelectrode to probe the exposed brain of a fully awake woman. Since the brain has no pain receptors, the patient calmly responded to the sensations she felt as Penfield touched different parts of her brain. At one point, the woman heard music and began to hum the theme to a concert she had attended as a child.

"Penfield's research suggests that memories from our early life are recorded in the brain," writes Hunter. "While we may have forgotten sights, sounds, and intense personal experiences, nonetheless they are permanently recorded in our magnificent brain. We may hear a song or smell a particular odor and an event will come rushing back."[3]

Our brains are storehouses for memories. We can choose to create soul-nourishing memories for our children. We can choose to help them "remember the Lord, who is great and awesome," (Neh. 4:14) and "remember the wonders he has done" (1 Chron. 16:12).

Using the celebrations in this book will help you create memories for teaching your children God's Word.

minutes *versus* moments

minutes	moments
Focus is task oriented	Focus is relationship oriented
Take life from us	Give life to us
Enter time	Are timeless
Nurture habits	Nurture hearts
Move us to be fully preoccupied	Move us to be fully present
Lived in integrity form character	Lived in intimacy transform hearts
Keep order with to-do lists	Bring divine order and beauty
Live life in your head	Live life from your heart
Consume our passions	Celebrate our passions

remember me

In the Book of Deuteronomy, God constantly exhorts His people to remember. The Book of Judges describes the awesome miracles of God shown to three generations of Israelites starting with Moses' generation.

The parents told the second-generation children stories of God's supernatural feats including the parting of the Red Sea and the defeat of Pharaoh. Dinnertime conversations and bedtime stories explained the significance of the Ten Commandments written by the finger of God.

But something happened with the third generation, the grandchildren of those whose feet trekked across the Red Sea on dry ground. Josh McDowell and Bob Hostetler, in their book *Right From Wrong*, explain the erosion of the Israelites' rich spiritual legacy:

The third generation of free Israelites grew up not knowing the Lord nor the things He had done for Israel because . . . while their parents gave them many material blessings, they did not do as their parents before them had done.

They neglected to tell their children the stories of how God had led them out of Egypt and had given them victory after victory over their enemies. They failed to repeat, over and over again, how God had given them the Law, and why His commands were so important.

The mothers taught their daughters how to beat soiled linen on the river rocks; the fathers emphasized the importance of bringing in the crop; but they never got around to teaching God's precepts to their children.

They had camels to trade, barns to build, parties to plan, weddings to attend—a hundred things to do—*but moral and spiritual instruction never made its way into their busy schedules.*[4]

Because of busyness and day-to-day activities, the third-generation Israelites "never got around to teaching God's precepts to their children." How easy it is to let daily demands crowd out the precious *kairos* moments with our children. The moments of answering "Daddy, does God sleep on the clouds?" and "Mommy, why can't I see Jesus right now?"

affecting the taste

In Greek, "beauty" means "ripened in God's time." We reflect God's beauty as we create moments with our children. The best way to tie our children's heartstrings to the truth is to create the moment of celebration, a moment when God enters in.

Just as God admonished the children of Israel in Deuteronomy 6:4-9, He counsels us:

Hear, O Israel: The LORD our God, the LORD is one. Love the LORD your God with all your heart and with all your

soul and with all your strength. These commandments that
I give you today are to be upon your hearts. Impress them
on your children. Talk about them when you sit at home
and when you walk along the road, when you lie down and
when you get up. Tie them as symbols on your hands and
bind them on your foreheads. Write them on the door-
frames of your houses and on your gates.

Verse 7 in the *Kings James Version* says, "Teach them diligently" to
your children. The Hebrew for "teach" is *lämad*, which means the
rod, to goad or instruct, to be skillful, an expert. Hebrew for "diligently" is *sha-nan,* which means to pierce, inculcate, sharpen, or
whet (drip by drip). We are to instruct our children so God's truth
moment by moment penetrates their hearts and minds.

Proverbs 22:6 (NASB) directs us to, "Train up a child in the way
he should go, even when he is old he will not depart from it." The
Hebrew for "train up" is *chanak,* which means to narrow, initiate,
discipline, create a desire. Train up also means to affect the taste. It
is a word picture of the Hebrew mother chewing up food and placing it on the palate of her baby.

As life-giving nurturers, we have the responsibility to affect the
taste of our children. This very day we are affecting the taste of the
next generation. We can affect their taste for convenience, entertainment, comfort, and discontent, or we can affect their taste for
the deep things of God. What an awesome gift and responsibility!

The following chapters show you ways to create a taste for the
things of the Spirit and ways to lead your children to the
Scriptures. Together we'll walk through practical ways to give three
life-empowering gifts to your children:

* The Gift of Perspective—teaching them to remember.
* The Gift of Purpose—why God created them.
* The Gift of Protection—setting spiritual boundaries for
their life.

God knows

Savoring *kairos* times slows us down and gives us the ability to be fully present in enjoying the moment. When psychologist William Marsten asked three thousand people, "What do you live for?", he was shocked to discover that 97 percent were simply enduring the present moment, waiting for the future.[5]

Are you eager to live the present moments with your children, or are you just coping until the day they move out on their own? If you're reading these pages with a weary or overwhelmed heart from the everyday struggles of parenting—rest assured that God sees and He understands.

Day by day you are in your home battling it out for the king-dom of God. You're in a dead heat for righteousness. You can be applauded for waking up in the morning and saying, "I choose to walk with God today, and I choose to raise these children."

God knows all about the family you were raised in and your scars and broken places. God knows if you're crying over that teenager all night. He knows if you're praying over that wayward spouse. He knows if you alone shoulder the parenting responsibilities.

He knows if you lack spiritual leadership in your home. He knows when you're up at night praying over your precious chil-dren. No matter what the twisted and tiring turns in your journey, God has tremendous plans for you as a parent. You are partnering with your Heavenly Father to bring His truth to your sons and daughters, and someday, their sons and daughters.

standing firm against all odds

Psalm 11:3 (NASB) asks, "If the foundations are destroyed, what can the righteous do?" We can rebuild secure foundations one brick at a time. God, your Master Builder, has a blueprint of success for each of your children. Our desire is to assist you in laying a solid spiritual base for your children one brick at a time.

The families working alongside Nehemiah to rebuild

Jerusalem's temple wall faced grueling opposition from local offi-
cials. A political, racial, and religious war pitted Nehemiah and the
Jews against the Samaritans, Arabians, Ammonites, and Ashdodites.

Furious townspeople hurled ridicule, insults, and jeers at the
workers and threatened military assaults. Yet Nehemiah and
Jehovah's people set their minds on the task entrusted to them.

We read of the people's tenacity in Nehemiah 4:13-14:

> Therefore I stationed some of the people behind the lowest
> points of the wall at the exposed places, posting them by
> *families*, with their swords, spears and bows. . . . I stood up
> and said . . . "Remember the Lord, who is great and awe-
> some, and fight for your brothers, your sons and your
> daughters, your wives and your homes."

Nehemiah didn't call for the bravest warriors, the strongest
men, the wisest politicians to stand—he called for *families* to stand
at the *exposed* places of the wall. Nehemiah directed the fathers and
mothers to stand firm against all odds. Where are we standing as
families today? Do we have the courage to stand at the exposed
places of our culture and fight for our sons and daughters? Are we
remembering that "the Lord, who is great and awesome" is leading
the charge?

"Certainly, the realm of parenting the next generation of God's
own is no place for the faint of heart," writes the author of *Proactive
Parenting*.[6] Parenting is not a dress rehearsal. Being wise parents is the
hardest thing we will ever do, but it is the highest calling. Will you
stand with us in giving everything we can for the next generation?

the best life worth living

President Theodore Roosevelt summed up the family's effect
on the entire nation in his 1907 annual address to Congress, "When
home ties are loosened, when men and women cease to regard a
worthy family life, with all its duties fully performed and all its
responsibilities lived up to, as the best life worth living, then evil

days for the [nation] are at hand."[7]

As you work day-to-day at modeling "the best life worth living" to your children, remember that God has gone before you. You don't need to be a super parent, just a parent who is open to learning from God and others.

We pray that the stories throughout this book will encourage your family to remember and rehearse the great things of God. Because this book describes living out *Celebrations of Faith* with our children, allow us to briefly introduce them to you:

Lauren—victorious one, our beautiful princess.
Colten—responsible, noble, leader, our righteous warrior.
Khrystian—free spirit, Christ-indwelt, our joyous wonder.
Jordan—life-giver, flowing river, our compassionate flower.
Logan—man of honor, our dramatic son, who loves to pray.
Kameryn—beloved one, our five-dimple beauty, who sings
    praises to God.

We trust that our *Celebrations of Faith* with our children will inspire you to cherish your special moments with your children. And when you create your own family celebrations, we'd love to hear about them. Your family traditions and rituals extend God's grace to your children.

Please understand that we've developed our family traditions over nearly twenty years of marriage and raising children. We did not adopt these celebrations overnight. With full schedules, sick kids, school, work, ministry, and church activities, and everything else in your life, it may work for you to choose one or two celebrations and do them consistently.

We all have a rhythm of life that is unique to our family, and the key to making the *Celebrations of Faith* work is picking a celebration that fits into the natural flow of your family life.

Just as dozens of wise mentors have poured into our lives to guide us in passing on a spiritual legacy to our children, we want to be here for you. As you adopt selected celebrations from those we share in the following chapters, you will be shaping the character and the decisions of your children for generations to come. You will tie each child's heartstrings to God's truth. What a privilege, what an adventure

🌸 What do I want my children to know about my heart?
✤ What do I want them to know about the heart of God?
❀ How can I better listen to the heartbeats of my children?
❀ What is one thing I can do to create a *kairos* moment with my family?

Father God, Elohim, I humbly bow before You as a needy parent dependent on You. I feel so inadequate to embrace the gift of time and use it wisely with my precious children. As I watch time disappear in the face of a three year old turning four, I wonder if I did enough this year to teach this little one about Your majesty. Help me listen to the heart-beats of my children. Please redeem our minutes. By Your grace, may our lives reflect the sanctuary of moments.

2

A Mother's Legacy

> **"**To preside there with such skill
> that husband and children will
> rise up and call her blessed is
> nobler than to rule an empire.**"**
> —*Harriet Beecher Stowe's mother*[1]

"Whad she doin'?" the blond-haired boy blurts out, peeking from behind the couch.

"Shhhhh . . . she's meetn' with Jesus," whispers the pig-tailed girl kneeling at his side.

Across the room near the window drenched in morning sun, a woman in a rocking chair snuggles under a multicolored green afghan. In one hand is a coffee mug and in the other an open *Living Bible*. Occasionally the woman pauses to look up with a slight contented smile on her sunlit face.

That's how I remember my mother first thing in the morning. For thirty years my mother ran a daycare in her home for healthy children, autistic children, children with cancer—children that no one else knew how to help.

As we got ready for school and Mom's baby-sitting customers arrived, we'd find Mom in the rocker by the living room window. Slowly sipping her coffee, Mom would ponder the Word, underlining verses that God impressed upon her heart. Mom loved sitting in her cozy rocker and soaking in God's goodness.

The little children in Mom's daycare would go home and imitate her. They'd sit in a rocker with a blanket and a cup and pick up any book that looked like my mom's Bible. They wanted to be like Mom. I wanted to be like her.

Now that I'm a mom, I'm passing on that baton of truth and tradition of reading God's Word to my own children. I used to spend time reading my Bible before my little ones were awake. But one day I realized they were not seeing me read God's Word as I saw my mother do.

I don't have a rocker by the window, so I sit at the kitchen table with my own little ones running in and out of the room saying, "Mommy! Are you being with Jesus?"

"Yes," I reply softly, sipping my coffee and smiling at the goodness of my God.

I am modeling to my children what their grandmother taught me: "Know therefore that the LORD your God is God; he is the faithful God, keeping his covenant of love to a thousand generations of those who love him and keep his commands" (Deut. 7:9).

I thank my mom for loving me by loving God first. My mom always said to me as a little girl, "Lisa, stand up straight. Put your shoulders back. When you walk into a room, you are a princess of the King. You are royalty."

So at a very young age, I asked Jesus to direct my life, and I delighted to know Him better. By third grade, I was a little obnoxious. At recess I'd bypass the others kids' invitation to play dodge ball so I could climb to the top of the monkey bars in my cat-eyed glasses and share the Gospel with a classmate. God called my little heart to know Him, and I was eager to be His servant.

If you think your children are too young to be tapped by God, you're wrong. God is wooing them to Himself, and we need to believe God can and will use them greatly. We need to partner with God in raising our children to follow Him all the days of their lives.

but God saw

My mother always told me that I was set apart for the Lord. She loved the name Lisa, but she didn't know that it meant "a consecrated gift, set apart to God." By His sustaining grace, I come from a rich legacy of women set apart for Him.

In the late 1800s, in a tiny Tennessee town, my great-great-grandmother was born. Haddie's arrival went unnoticed by the rest of the world, but God saw. She was born to near destitute cotton farmers, working all of her young life on a cotton farm just to survive.

Haddie married a young cotton farmer and they moved to a homestead in southern Missouri. Haddie Joslin delivered eight children, but five of them died from a severe intestinal virus before they were three years old. Haddie clung to God as her refuge through the deaths of her five toddlers. Haddie worked the cotton farm all day. At night she quilted and sang to her Lord and poured out her heart before Him.

In 1898, Nanny Joslin was born and her arrival went unnoticed by the rest of the world, but God saw. Nanny was full of life and love, and just like her mother, she grew full of faith. My great-grandmother Nanny married a Mr. Jordan and they had two sons. I knew my great-grandmother Nanny and remember her always wearing a calico apron and laughing so hard that her glasses would steam up.

Although Nanny had nothing in this world, she had her God. Nanny chose joy in mothering, and she chose to exalt God. Nanny touched me deeply as her great-granddaughter.

In 1923, a baby girl was born to the Pattersons, a God-fearing couple in southern Missouri. Addie Mae's arrival went unnoticed by the rest of the world, but God saw. Addie Mae used her beautiful voice to sing for her Lord, and she married Nanny's son, my grandfather.

In 1939, Addie Mae gave birth to the first of her four children—my mother, Sharon. Mom's arrival, too, went unnoticed by the rest of the world, but God saw. Grandma Addie Mae died of a blood disease at the age of thirty, leaving four children twelve and under. But right up until the time she died, my grandmother was telling others of her faith in Christ.

You can imagine the sorrow of leaving your young ones behind, yet Addie Mae found comfort in her God. Addie Mae's daughter, Sharon, married a Mr. Ramsey at age sixteen and gave birth to me in 1959. My arrival went unnoticed by the rest of the world, but God saw.

God is thinking of us

Mother had three babies before she was twenty-one. And when my father left, Mom clung to her God and the God of her mother, grandmother, and great-grandmother. These women's lives state clearly that anything that life hurls at us can be handed over to a living God, and He will sustain us.

But do you think that for more than 120 years these women were getting up every morning and living their lives and thinking of me, five generations down the line? Do you think they were saying to themselves, *I've got to be faithful for my great-great-grandchild. I've got to be faithful for her children. I've got to be faithful for generations to come?*

I don't think so. *But God was thinking of me*, and God is thinking of you, and God is thinking of your children. Every day the women in my family could have said, "I'm too young to die. God can't be a loving God." They could have quit. They could have said, "I've lost too many children. God is not faithful." They could have said, "I don't have a faithful husband. I quit." But none of them quit.

My great-great-grandmother loved God. My great-grandmother loved Him. My grandmother and my mother loved Him. And I love Him. And by God's grace, my children will love Him. No matter what circumstances you face, you, too, can choose to love God and teach your children to love Him.

About a year into our marriage, I encountered troubling nightmares that Randy would leave me. Because my own father left our family when I was one, the heartache from that abandonment was handed down to me. But with each nightmare, Randy reassured me, "Honey, I will never, ever, ever, leave you. Ever."

Eventually my fearful nightmares subsided, but it wasn't until a few years later that God revealed something significant to me. About the time my mother was born, a baby girl was born to an Ohio couple. Vivian grew into a free-spirited outdoor girl who boasted that she loved horses and God—and in that order. Her heart's desire was to become a godly woman and raise a godly family.

God heard Vivian's prayers and blessed her with a husband and six children. In 1958, nine months before I was born, Vivian gave birth to a son. His name is Randy, which means "loyal one, protector." God named Randy Wilson in his mother's womb and set him apart for twenty-three years before he married me. What incredible grace!

Before Randy was born, God was thinking of me. He knew I would someday need a faithful man to be my loyal protector. God met me at my biggest fear by naming a boy in the womb who is committed to be there for me. Even before your children are born, God has already planned their generation with a future and a hope (Jer. 29:11).

the language we speak

The language of women brings life or death. The language of just a handful of feminists changed the spiritual genetics of this country for the past forty years. While God does promise us a hopeful future, the Enemy still lurks about seeking to destroy individuals, families, and homes. One of his attacks in our society is the poisonous language and attitude challenging the significance of women and mothers.

Author Iris Krasnow recalls a visit to an advertising executive who four days before had given birth and was planning to return to work full time the following week:

She was propped up in bed talking on a telephone that was

wedged in the crook of her neck. With one hand she was holding her child to her breast, the other hand was clutching a fax just in. The phone call about a client dispute was getting her riled and she started swatting the air with the hand that had seconds earlier been securing her newborn. The baby dropped into the sea of papers that covered her bed, and as my friend ranted on, there her daughter lay, with black ink smudged on her cheek.

In observing this new mother's priorities, Krasnow adds ". . . there's nothing we can do more powerful as women than refuse to abandon motherhood."[2] Unfortunately, many women today abandon motherhood. Many exchange the beauty of a woman's nurturing heart for restlessness, resentment, and rage.

What language are we speaking? Our culture has turned beautiful spirits into fighting spirits. And we've passed our discontented attitudes and harsh words on to our children. But we can bind up the poisonous language and loose the loving, powerful truth of God's language, not only in our own hearts, but also in our children's hearts.

In *Generations: The History of America's Future*, a secular documentary on America's heritage, the authors write that the personality of each generation is established by "in particular, the attitudes of women and mothers toward their own sex roles and their family roles. . . . [These roles] are central to a generation's peer personality."[3]

Women's attitudes—how we feel about our place in our society—set the entire personality for this generation. The Bible warns about generations that follow their fleshly desires and turn their backs on God. Jesus describes these people as a "faithless and perverse generation" (Matt. 17:17, KJV). What will He say about our generation? And what will He say about us as women . . . as mothers?

faithful mothers

I'm writing this to give you a new vision of the power of women. I want to encourage you in your divine uniqueness. As a mother, you were designed by God with a nurturing heart to love your children.

Let's take a look at some other women through the centuries who influenced their children's children for generations. In the 1700s, three ordinary women got up every morning in their ordinary homes and said, "I walk with God." They had no radio, no faxes, no e-mails. They probably never knew that each other existed. But God knew.

One was Susanna Wesley. She lived in England and gave birth to nineteen children. Eleven of them lived. Two of her boys—Charles and Jonathan—transformed the history of Europe and America.

Some mean-spirited folk threatened Susanna and her children because of their faith and even attempted to burn down the Wesleys' house. Susanna's husband was away much of the time, yet this courageous mother trained her children day after day in the Scriptures.

You may think, *How bad were the 1700s for Susanna Wesley?* When asked about raising children, Susanna Wesley once said, "No one can, without renouncing the world, in the most literal sense, observe my method; and *there are few, if any, that would entirely devote above twenty years of the prime of life in hopes to save the souls of their children.*"[4]

In her day, Susanna could not find women who would devote themselves to their children. Sadly, many women today share this same perspective. About the time Susanna was raising her family, a woman in America named Mary gave birth to a boy named George. George Washington was a year old when twenty-nine-year-old John Wesley brought his message to America. With the Great Awakening underway, Mary and Augustine Washington were touched by the power of God, and the moral fiber of our country solidified to usher in the revolution.

Another mother, Sarah Edwards, a dazzling beauty in brocade suits, determined with her husband, Jonathan, to raise their eleven children according to the Scriptures.

You may think, *In the 1700s, how bad could the culture be?*

Jonathan Edwards describes many of the children of that day as "infinitely more hateful than a generation of vipers."[5] These children were totally out of control, running the streets, and wildly downing alcohol. But Sarah Edwards from the safe haven of her home declared, "Not my children. They belong to God."

These three women, Susanna, Mary, and Sarah, partnered with a mighty God and helped set afire the Great Awakening in our country. Historians agree that without this great spiritual revival, no political revolution would have freed our nation. The sweeping change in the moral fabric of America started with faithful mothers in quiet homes who loved God and their children.

legacy of influence

In spite of the lack of encouragement from the women of her day, and in spite of the "vipers" taunting her children, Sarah Edwards persevered. And God honored her prayers and her commitment.

When A.E. Winship studied 1,400 of Sarah's descendants, he discovered that the Edwards produced:

Thirteen college presidents.
Sixty-five professors.
One hundred lawyers and a dean of a law school.
Thirty judges.
Fifty-six physicians and a dean of a medical school.
Eighty holders of public office:
    Three United States Senators.
    Three mayors of large cities.
    Three governors of large states.
    One comptroller of the U.S. Treasury.
    One vice president of the United States.[6]

Winship credited much of the capacity, talent, intensity, and character of the 1,400 Edwards family members to Sarah. Because of this tenacious mother's absolute love for the Lord and His Word, generation after generation of her children's children tackled great things for God and their world.

World history changed forever when this one mom set aside *kairos* moments with her children. She obeyed the voice of her God and not the voice of her culture. Scripture tells us of many faith-filled women whose children grew up and changed history. Moses, Samuel, and Timothy are three bold leaders raised by righteous mothers.

The Apostle Paul commends Timothy's heritage: "I have been reminded of your sincere faith, which first lived in your grand-mother Lois and in your mother Eunice and, I am persuaded, now lives in you also" (2 Tim. 1:5).

God wants to use the faith living in you to work in the souls of your children. Are you willing to let Him work?

tender words in the desert

After Randy and I married, I had six pregnancies in four years, which I thought was impossible. I was pregnant, nursing, miscarry-ing, and chasing three toddlers in diapers. We lost two babies, and I sank into depression. I would shut the drapes and take the phone off the hook. I showed up at church once a week with my make-up and hair done, but no one knew my despair. Most days I moaned, "God, I feel like I'm going to die." He responded, "Exactly. This is about your death and My resurrection. Because, My precious daughter, I don't need you for My kingdom, but I want to partner with you."

God took me through years of barren blackness, of not know-ing how I was going to make it. But one day He led me to the Book of Hosea. I lamented, "God, Hosea is about a prostitute. What does this have to do with my life?" I felt Him say, *"It has everything to do with your life."*

So I read Hosea 2:3, "I will make her like a desert, turn her into a parched land, and slay her with thirst." Have you ever had God slay you with thirst? I would open the Scriptures and feel nothing but despair. I didn't sense God's presence, and I just didn't know how I could go on.

But God was in the process of stripping me from performance Christianity and saying, "This is about My heart in you, and until you get it, we're not going to move."

As you read these pages, maybe you're in a desert place. Maybe God has slain you with thirst. In Hosea 2 God says that He leads us personally into the desert places. In verses 6 and 7 the Lord describes how He blocks this wayward woman's path with thorn-bushes and walls her in "so that she cannot find her way."

I jotted in my Bible that thorns are a "place of grace." Thorns are lovingly placed by God in our lives to bring pain that actually protects us from our *own* way and leads us to *His* way. I wanted things easy, and mothering took me to the very end of myself. Maybe that's where you are today. Fortunately, as we see in Hosea, God does not abandon us in our burned-out times. Just as He restored this hardened prostitute, He promises to nourish us:

> I will lead her into the desert and speak tenderly to her [the Hebrew says, "speak to her heart"]. There I will give her back her vineyards, and will make the Valley of Achor a door of hope. There she will sing as in the days of her youth, as in the day she came up out of Egypt (Hosea 2:14-15).

Sometimes God has to take us to the end of ourselves, because the desert places are where our songs and our fruit come forth, and where He speaks tenderly to our hearts. The desert can be a place of intimacy.

Maybe you're in a scorched place, and you don't see how God can refresh you and mightily use you as a parent. Isaiah 58:11 says, "The LORD will guide you always; he will satisfy your needs in a sun-scorched land and will strengthen your frame. You will be like a well-watered garden, like a spring whose waters never fail."

All of us have some hidden, scorched place—but God says, "I want to make Myself known and the most beautiful, powerful way is through your resting in Me in your mothering."

Colossians 1:17 says, "He is before all things, and in him all things hold together." Sometimes we are just at the end saying to ourselves, *I just can't go with one more sleepless night. I can't fight with that child one more time. God, I can't do it.* In spite of our ragged feelings, God is holding us together—every fiber of our being—in the palm of His hand.

In the Old Testament women would give their children to idols, and we read this and think, *How horrible! How could these mothers give their offspring to idols of fire?* But today we offer our own children to idols when we choose convenience over conviction . . . default over decision. Our children will become what we pour into them.

Even on our worst day, we must remember that we are still the apple of God's eye. Even on our worst day, we are still the delight of His heart. Even on our worst day, we are still His bright light in a fallen world. Wendy Brewer poignantly sums up God's presence in the tough days of motherhood:

> Today I didn't say the right things. I didn't give enough hugs. I didn't listen to all their imaginary stories. Today I hurried them through what could have been very special moments, to achieve my binding agenda. Today my prayers were too short and my lectures too long. My smiles, I'm sure, didn't hide my fatigue. Today I didn't heal any wounds; in fact, I'm sure I caused some. Their tears fell and I felt too lifeless to wipe them away. Today I felt completely defeated and totally inadequate for this position called "mommy." But as I kneel in prayer to confess my failures, I am reminded . . . I am not their hope. I am not their total joy. I am not their salvation. He is![7]

Some days we may feel like failures as mothers, but let's not forget that just as God saw the tenacious lives of Susanna, Mary, Sarah, Haddie, Nanny, Addie Mae, and Sharon, He is standing with us this very day.

A great awakening lies in the heart of every mother who will say "yes" to God. He only needs one!

❀ Who are the women in my life who have helped shape my soul?

❀ What kind of legacy do I want to leave for my children?

❀ How can I stay strong when I face tough times?

❀ What women in history do I see as models?

❀ Have I thanked the women who have guided my heart?

Thank You, Lord, for creating me and giving me a rich heritage in You. Take my past, my present, and my future and use all my days to influence my children for Your glory. At times as a mother I feel overwhelmed and weary, but You see my every step. Take my weakness and make it Your strength. Open my heart to Your truths, so my children will learn of Your unending goodness no matter what circumstances come our way. May I always be faithful to You in all that I am and in all that I do. I love You. Amen.

3
The Father Warrior

> **" Anything less than a conscious commitment to the important is an unconscious commitment to the unimportant. "**
> —*Stephen Covey*[1]

One Memorial Day weekend on the slopes of Washington's Mount Rainier, Christian dentist James Reddick was teaching the joy of mountain hiking to his twelve-year-old daughter and eleven-year-old son. Suddenly a storm with battering hurricane-force winds and thick, blinding snow pelted them on the slopes.

With an aluminum mess kit, Reddick struggled to carve an oblong trench in the quickly accumulating snow. He wrapped his children in sleeping bags away from the tunnel's entrance and covered the opening with a tarp. The howling winds ripped at the makeshift door, exposing the trench to the frigid swirling snow. So to protect his daughter and son, Reddick lay across the opening and held the tarp down with his own weight.

Two days later, searchers spotted a corner of a backpack poking through the deep snow. Quickly digging away at the snow-covered mound, the team hoped to find the three missing hikers. They found Sharon and David chilled but alive. But their father's stiff body lay along one wall of the snow cave. In one searcher's words, this brave father had "taken the cold spot" by using his own back as the outer wall.[2]

Every day cultural storms rage around our children and seek to destroy their emotional and spiritual well-being. Do we see the storms coming? Are we willing to lay down our lives to block whatever harsh elements threaten the lives of our children? This chapter focuses on setting the course for fathers to overcome life's squalls and pass along a seasoned faith to our sons and daughters.

fathers are warriors

The Hebrew words for "manhood" in Scripture each describe seasons in a man's life. The word *gibbor* translates into English as "warrior." *Gibbor* or warrior also refers to the different types of warriors in the different seasons of life.

In Genesis the warrior is the mighty hunter.
The warrior in Psalms wins the race.
In 2 Kings, Boaz is the warrior of great wealth.
Joshua was the warrior of incredible physical and spiritual stamina.
The warriors in Judges were the elite combatants much like our Marines today.
The warriors in 2 Samuel were handpicked by David and enshrined in the "house of heroes."
The sixty warriors in Solomon's army stood as the noblest of Israel.

Yet the ultimate spiritual reward for the warrior is not in his honors, decorations, or medals, *but in the children God gave to him!*[3] Psalm 127:3-5 underscores this divine value placed on the family: "Sons are a heritage from the LORD, children a reward from him. Like arrows in the hands of a warrior are sons born in one's youth. Blessed is the man whose quiver is full of them. They will not be put to shame when they contend with their enemies in the gate."

God drafted you as a father warrior. As a warrior, your children are your real strength; they are your arrows. You are not a warrior in spite of your children, you are a warrior *because* of your children.

God, in creating the family, releases His fulfillment in fathers, as we take responsibility to fulfill this role. There is great depth of satisfaction and fulfillment in fathering a family. A picture of how fatherhood transforms a man is seen in the life of Warren Beatty. In a *Vanity Fair* article, the interviewer writes:

> Marriage has transformed Beatty, who speaks of his life as falling into two parts, "Before Annette" and "With Annette." [Beatty] elaborates, "When I was in my 20s and 30s, there were certain things that were irresistible." Pause. "And then into my 40s." He laughs, and pauses again. "And into my 50s. Being adolescent never got boring to me. And that fortunately came to a conclusion, not a moment too soon. I stood a good chance of reaching the end of my days as a solitary, eccentric . . . *fool.*[4]

For some fifty years, Beatty lived for himself warring for his own pleasure. He drifted, indulging in everything that pleased himself. Beatty's life changed when he married and had children. A warrior needs a purpose for which to war. Beatty realized this almost too late.

Fulfillment in fathering is a by-product of obedience, not an end to itself. Some of this fulfillment comes from building a strong relationship between the husband and wife. It also comes from walking with your children through their transitional stages of development. Children get their identity from their relationship with their dad. If your relationship with your wife is fractured, or you have not built a relationship with your children, your children will wander in search of who they are.

LIFE magazine tells the story of Steven Spielberg's strained relationship with his dad. The divorce of his parents created a profound effect on the powerhouse filmmaker. His movie *E.T. The Extra-Terrestrial* is "an accusatory yet plaintive letter to his father."

Spielberg explains, "The whole movie is really about divorce . . . Henry's ambition to find a father by bringing E.T. into his life to fill some black hole—that was my struggle to find somebody to replace the dad who I felt had abandoned me."[5]

needing guidance

David was like every other man in his generation. He grew up during the Depression, a hard-working, frugal man. David married, had six children, and endeavored to provide for his family. David took his family to church and visited and cared for his aging parents. His big heart had a difficult time saying no to his children's wants.

All of David's children grew up, graduated from high school, and married, delighting him with twenty-five grandchildren. David's life is a success story by today's standards. I am proud to be his son.

Looking back at Dad's life, I realize that his mind was focused on making more money so that he could make us more comfortable. That was his caring heart. But like most men of his day, Dad lacked guidance in how to father us *emotionally* and give us navigation skills in understanding life. Books and courses on parenting were not available to him and his generation as they are today.

Children take from the home what is lived out in the home. Your children are watching you and wondering: *Will Dad help me when I need it? Will Dad love me no matter what I do or fail to do?* Few men sign up for Fathering 101, but you can learn to be actively present with your children. You can learn to foster *kairos* moments with your family.

As a dad, it's important that you spend one-on-one time with your children looking deep into their eyes and into their worlds to find out what is important to them. Ask them: What is your greatest fear? What brings you the greatest joy? Part of your role is to teach your children that life is difficult, yet God carries and comforts us in this world. Your kids need to hear from you how everything in life rests in who God is and in our relationship with Him.

Some of my most meaningful interactions with my kids occur during everyday activities. I remember one particular time I was running to the store, and Lauren, who was about twelve years old at the time, asked to join me. During our drive to and from the store, Lauren opened up about some of her current struggles. When she paused, I asked questions to draw her out more.

I'll never forget Lauren's words as we walked back into the house that day. "Thank you, Dad, for spending that time with me. I just needed a few minutes with you so I could see life clearly again." We give our children new eyes to see when we give them our hearts that listen.

conscious commitment

Because Lisa and I did not have fathers who knew how to be fully invested in our hearts and everyday lives, after we were married we turned to godly men and women who helped coach us in our marriage and parenting skills. As new parents, we literally invited ourselves to the homes of people we viewed as successful parents, and with pad and pen in our hands we asked questions about their parenting.

God has etched in our hearts the desire to help other dads and moms develop parenting skills. In upcoming chapters, we will look at specific ways to create *kairos* moments with our family. And believe me, placing a high premium on my family did not come naturally! I was the jock who wanted to join the guys in a softball game as soon as I returned from my honeymoon. I played softball two or three nights a week, plus tournaments on the weekend. Not to mention playing on a basketball league and catching all the major sports on television as a break from running my own business.

Over the years, God slowly turned my heart away from my sports obsession to concentrate more on my family. I still love sports and coach my oldest son's hockey team, but I now see my family as my top priority.

Several years ago I chose to finish my college degree. During this time we had two babies in fifteen months and I was working two jobs. In evaluating how this decision could alter my time with my children, I committed to get up at 3:30 in the morning to study and write before work. I knew I had to take the weight of this heavy schedule on me, so that Lisa and the children would not feel the effects. After work I still enjoyed dinner and an evening with my family. The kids did not notice a shift in my schedule.

Was this easy? No! But as Oswald Chambers writes in *My Utmost for His Highest*, "If we are going to live as disciples of Jesus, we have to remember that all noble things are difficult."[6] God was my total sufficiency!

Looking back, those fully packed days seem like a blur, but God's grace was sufficient. He was my strength as Proverbs 10:29 (KJV) says, "The way of the LORD is strength to the upright." God worked in my heart to make this sacrifice for my family. But sacrifices are *investments*. I believe that when God calls you to do something, He provides, protects, and equips you with the desire, time, and resources.

taking the lead

The verb form of "father" means to author, to be a *founder* or the *foundation*. Fathering centers on originating, influencing, and sharpening. You are to take the lead in authoring or creating the "curriculum for life" for generations to come. God created you to be the pacesetter, the chief steward of your family's well-being.

The responsibility of fathering is tremendous. Many dads don't feel adequate to father their children. I understand that. There are many times I don't feel adequate either. The men in history who helped change our world often felt inadequate too. Moses and Jeremiah feared God's call to leadership because they felt "slow of speech and tongue" (Ex. 4:10, Jer. 1:6). Presidents Washington and Adams wrote of feeling unqualified to meet the challenge of shaping America's government.

None of these men felt fit for the task. Yet these men and fathers pressed through their fears and hesitancies to affect the lives of future generations, and so must we. God reassures us in Philippians 4:13, "I can do everything through Him who gives me strength."

God handpicked us to live in this generation, and God handpicked us as father warriors for our children. Ken Canfield spurs us onward when he writes, "Just because circumstances have become more difficult does not mean that my responsibilities have changed. *Fathers father.* Committed fathers do their duty. Effective fathers find ways to be effective in the face of adversity and discouragement."[7]

If you consider yourself a weak warrior for your family, do not wallow in guilt or self-condemnation. God is walking right alongside you to guide you in your fathering. Connect with other men and help each other walk through the struggles of fathering together. By God's grace He will help you as He has helped me.

Perhaps you are looking for practical ways to be the father God designed you to be. Great! Keep reading. The rest of this book gives you proven helps on how to safeguard and shepherd your family and cultivate meaningful memories with your children.

"get up" and "stand up"

The Bible speaks to women with gentleness and compassion, but to men in terms of "get up," "stand up," "go forward." In Judges 7:9 God speaks to Gideon in the middle of the night about fighting against Midian, "*Get up*, go down against the camp, because I am going to give it into your hands."

When Elijah despairs of life and hides in the desert, an angel wakens Elijah from his sleep, "*Get up* and eat" (1 Kings 19:5). In the Garden of Gethsemane, Jesus directs his sleepy disciples, "*Get up* and pray so that you will not fall into temptation" (Luke 22:46).

We also find God commanding Joshua, "*Stand up!* What are you doing down on your face?" (Josh. 7:10), and in Jeremiah 1:17 God tells the weeping prophet, Jeremiah, "Get yourself ready! *Stand up* and say to them whatever I command you."

Are you ready to get up and stand up as a father warrior? The father in the opening story was a warrior who gave his life in protecting his son and daughter. Father warrior, are you covering the exposed places that pose a danger for your children? Are you standing as the warrior, the *gibbor* at the gates of your home protecting your family from culture's assault to pillage your children's emotional, physical, and spiritual purity? As a father you must war against all that crowds your life inside the home and all that pulls you outside the home: career, sports, or an over-committed, exhausting schedule that gives your best to others—rather than to your family.

Perhaps your career drains you of the energy and time you'd like to devote to your children. At the end of the day, your kids get a few scraps of the leftover you. "Crowded lives produce fatigue—and fatigue produces irritability," notes psychologist James Dobson, "and irritability produces indifference—and indifference can be interpreted by the child as a lack of genuine affection and personal esteem."[8]

Is fatigue and irritability putting the squeeze on your relationships with your family? If so, what is one step you can take this week to regain healthy communication with your children? Stu Weber in *Tender Warrior* says, "Nothing makes up for the failure of a family. At the heart of a real man's vision is the health of his family."[9] How would you describe the health of your family?

A turn-of-the-century Yiddish poem that appeared in the *Wall Street Journal* summarizes the need for fathers to be present in our children's everyday lives:

I have a son, a little son,
A boy completely fine.
When I see him it seems to me
That all the world is mine.
But seldom, seldom do I see
My child awake and bright;
I only see him when he sleeps;

I'm only home at night.
It's early when I leave for work;
When I return it's late.
Unknown to me is my own flesh,
Unknown is my child's face.
When I come home so wearily
In the darkness after day,
My pale wife exclaims to me:
"You should have seen our child play."
I stand beside his little bed,
I look and try to hear.
In his dream he moves his lips:
"Why isn't Papa here?"[10]

Will you commit to being a Papa who is there for *your* children?

fighting the good fight

As Abraham Lincoln once declared, "Your war will not be won by strategy alone, but more by hard, desperate fighting."[11] Whether you realize it or not, you are in a battle for your children's attention and affections. God has chosen you to defend your family from the Enemy's ploys.

You may feel somewhat inadequate or overwhelmed in taking a stronger stand as a father, but courage is not the absence of fear, it is pressing through fear. God wants you to press through any fears you may have about parenting. He promises you in Proverbs 29:25, "Fear of man will prove to be a snare, but whoever trusts in the LORD is kept safe." As the leader of your family, you can trust in the Lord who keeps you safe to give you guidance each step of the way.

You can also hang on to the sage advice of tenacious Teddy Roosevelt, who in 1910 delivered this address in Sorbonne, Paris:

> It is not the critic who counts: not the man who points out
> how the strong man stumbled or where the doer of deeds
> could have done them better: The credit belongs to the
> man who is actually in the arena: whose face is marred by

> the dust and sweat. . . . Far better it is to dare mighty things, to win glorious triumphs even though checkered by failure, than to rank with those poor spirits who neither enjoyed nor suffer much because they live in the gray twilight that knows neither victory nor defeat.[12]

You are in the fatherhood arena. Your face may be grimy with dust and sweat, but you are daring to take God at His Word and stand up for your children. I and thousands of other fathers are standing right along with you.

As fathers, we are called to be warriors and to "fight the good fight" (1 Tim. 1:18). This is a battle we must win at all cost. I challenge you to stand and fight with me as a victorious father warrior. *This* is holy ground.

personal reflection

- What kind of warrior am I? In what areas am I waging war?
- In what area do I excel as a father?
- In what area of fathering do I need the greatest improvement?
- How do my days reflect my heart as a father?
- Is there anything in my life (unforgiveness, bitterness, anger, fatigue, pride, insensitivity) that is blocking my relationship with my family?
- Am I willing to humble myself and ask my wife to forgive me for areas in which I've acted as a weak warrior? Am I willing to do the same with my children?
- Who is one man who can mentor me as a father?

personal prayer

Lord, thank You for being my *Jehovah Sabaoth*—the Lord of Hosts, the Warfare God. Thank You for being intimately acquainted with all my ways and modeling how to be a warring, caring father. Help me overcome my unbelief in being the dad you created me to be. Replace my doubts with Your determination, my fears with Your might. Move me from the gray twilight into Your victorious light. Strengthen my weak areas as a father warrior to my family. Open my eyes to learn from You and from others around me. Empower me with the courage and commitment to stand up for my family, so that some day, generation after generation of my children will take a stand for You too. May I war for noble things. Amen.

A father is someone who
walks a path in a way that attracts others to want to walk the same path.

A father is someone who
occasionally turns around and looks on his children following behind with a compassion that leaves no doubt he understands and cares what life is like for them. He understands because he has taken the time to listen to them and because he hasn't forgotten his own history; he cares because he feels deeply how much he longs for what is not yet his.

A father is someone who
turns again to face ahead, away from his children, and continues his journey, never giving help that would allow his children to succeed easily—and thereby weaken their character. By living for something more important than his children, a father gives them the most precious gift any father can give—the gift of transcendence. His ongoing involvement with them keeps them from feeling abandoned and worthless. His passion for God keeps them from thinking they are the center of life. Instead, they are drawn to join him in pressing on toward the highest goal. [13]

—Dr. Larry Crabb, Jr.

PART TWO

The Gift of Perspective

4
The Grace of Remembering

One summer morning right after Logan was born, our other
children were acting cranky and needed more discipline and time
than Lisa could muster. Feeling exhausted by company and the
adjustments to a new little one, Lisa put Logan down for a nap,
grabbed her Bible and told the kids, "Mommy needs some time
with God alone. I'll be back shortly."

When Lisa walked back in the house from sitting on the front
porch, our oldest two, Lauren and Colten, came running and shouting, "Mommy, come here!" Grabbing Lisa's hand they excitedly led
her upstairs to our bedroom.

Hundreds of white lights from our Christmas tree dangled
from the ceiling. Lisa's honeymoon gown, wedding flowers, and
pearl necklace adorned our bed. Candles glowed around the room,
and soft instrumental music created a soothing ambiance.

"Mommy, sit down," Lauren and Colten pleaded as Lisa stood
tearfully overwhelmed by the tender insight of our children.
"Mommy, we know that we've had bad attitudes, and we've been

struggling in getting along. And you're very tired. But you know what? When we get to heaven, you'll never be tired, and we'll never have attitudes. So please forgive us for our attitudes this morning. We decorated your room like heaven so you would have a place to rest. We just wanted you to remember how wonderful heaven is going to be!"

How precious our children were to create heaven in our bedroom and ask forgiveness for a rough day. How wonderful that they wanted to create something that would help us both remember the goodness of our God and a bit of heaven on earth. How blessed we all are with the grace of remembering.

thankful hearts

When we started having children we never sat down and said, "We need to do some really cute things to remind our little ones about God." We would just go to the Scriptures and say, "How can we make this a moment instead of a minute? How can we tie our children's hearts to this truth?" Over time God began to give us what we've come to call *Celebrations of Faith*. We divide these celebrations into three overall gifts: the gift of perspective, the gift of purpose, and the gift of protection.

We begin with the gift of perspective—teaching our children to remember. The foundation of remembering is a grateful heart. When God says He hates sins such as murder, idolatry, and slander, He also includes *unthankfulness*, a sign of a proud heart (2 Timothy 3:2-5). In the Old Testament, Jehovah warns the children of Israel against pride and forgetfulness:

> Be careful that you do not forget the LORD your God. . . .
> Otherwise, when you eat and are satisfied, when you build
> fine houses and settle down, and when your herds and
> flocks grow large and your silver and gold increase and all
> you have is multiplied, then your heart will become proud
> and you will forget the LORD your God (Deut. 8:11-14).

When we grow comfortable and complacent in life, we can forget to thank God. Unthankfulness takes root in our children's souls if we don't teach them to remember God and His provisions. If our children get to the point where they don't remember, or we're not creating moments for them to remember, they will become hard and proud because remembering cultivates gratitude and a humble heart.

God wants our hearts "overflowing with thankfulness" (Col. 2:7), and He counsels us in Deuteronomy 4:9 to "watch yourselves closely so that you do not forget the things your eyes have seen or let them slip from your heart as long as you live. Teach them to your children and to their children after them." Teaching our children to remember gives them the gift of perspective and the meaning of life through understanding their past and their spiritual heritage.

gaining perspective

Remembering who God is and what He has done for us keeps our hearts bowed in reverence toward God and breeds thankfulness and humility. This is the richest soil we can ask for in the hearts of our children and each other.

Remembering gives us the perspective to be reverent. "I will remember the deeds of the LORD, yes, I will remember your miracles of long ago. I will meditate on all your works and consider all your mighty deeds" (Ps. 77:11-12).

Remembering gives us the perspective to be courageous and not give in to fear. "You may say to yourselves, 'These nations are stronger than we are. How can we drive them out?' But do not be afraid of them; remember well what the LORD your God did to Pharaoh and to all Egypt" (Deut. 7:17-18).

Remembering gives us perspective in our trials. "Remember how the LORD your God led you all the way in the desert these forty years, to humble you and to test you in order to know what was in your heart, whether or not you would keep his commands" (Deut. 8:2).

Remembering gives us perspective that keeps us from sin and sobers our judgment. "Remember Lot's wife! Whoever tries to keep his life will lose it, and whoever loses his life will preserve it" (Luke 17:32-33).

What happens when we forget? Psalm 78 shows us the cycle of forgetting and remembering. Remembering leads to *life*, forgetting leads to *death*.

Forgetting leads to fear. "The men of Ephraim, though armed with bows, turned back on the day of battle; they did not keep God's covenant and refused to live by his law. They forgot what he had done, the wonders he had shown them." (Ps. 78:9-11).

Forgetting leads to rebellion. "But they continued to sin against him, rebelling in the desert against the Most High" (Ps. 78:17).

Forgetting leads to pride. "They willfully put God to the test by demanding the food they craved. They spoke against God, saying, 'Can God spread a table in the desert?'" (Ps. 78:18-19).

Forgetting stirs up the anger of God. "God's anger rose against them; he put to death the sturdiest among them, cutting down the young men of Israel" (Ps. 78:31).

Forgetting leads to disbelief. "In spite of all this, they kept on sinning; in spite of his wonders, they did not believe" (Ps. 78:32).

God embraces symbols and ceremonies

God loves and commands remembering. He sets the example Himself—with symbols. In His blessing to Noah, He says:

> "And I will remember My covenant, which is between Me and you and every living creature of all flesh; and never again shall the water become a flood to destroy all flesh. When the bow is in the cloud, then I will look upon it, to remember the everlasting covenant between God and every living creature of all flesh that is on the earth. . . . This is

the sign of the covenant which I have established between
Me and all flesh that is on the earth" (Gen. 9:15-17, NASB).

Throughout Scripture we see God using symbols and ceremonies to teach the "children and their children after them." Some
of God's object lessons include: stones, a pillar of fire, a cloud,
manna, the ark of the covenant, a dove, an olive branch, and writ-
ings on doorposts. God loves ceremonies. He loves blessings. He
loves sacrifices of repentance and the anointings of kings.

He talks about ceremonies and celebrations including the
Passover, the Sabbath, and the Lord's Supper. All of these symbols
and practices were set up to help His forgetful children remember.

How does one generation get the truth of God to the next? By
constantly repeating and rehearsing the goodness of God. We have
heard it said, "We are only one generation away from atheism." God
uses *families*, one person at a time to present His glorious truth.

But we are such a forgetful people! It is interesting to note that
in Exodus 14 and 15, the Israelites witnessed the incredible miracle
of crossing of the Red Sea, and *immediately* went from miracle to
murmuring and from praise to pouting in the desert.

Instantly after a huge miracle, they *forgot* what God had done.
God gave His people manna and knew that they would eat it three
times a day for forty years and they would still *forget* how He took
care of them. In Exodus 16:33, they were told to put a jar full of
manna in the ark of the covenant. Manna means "What is it?" They
did not even know what to call it. They ate "what is it" for forty
years, but God knew they would still forget!

How forgetful we all are! If we as parents don't *purposefully* set
in place the symbols and celebrations that point our children to
God, they will *make their own*.

Just look at the story of God's chosen people in Exodus. The
stubborn Israelites forgot their God as their leader Moses met with
Jehovah on Mount Sinai to receive the Ten Commandments. It only
took forty days for the Israelites to forget all that God had done.
With their minds off God, they asked Aaron to help them create a

false god, a golden calf. And in Romans 1 we read how people continued to forget God, created their own images, and grew depraved
in their own minds.

Forgetting is serious business. It leads to unthankfulness and a
lack of reverence for God, and destroys His work for generations to
come. We must give our children the gift of perspective by teaching
them to reverently remember. We as parents must celebrate and
choose what symbols and ceremonies we will build memories
around for our children. They must be founded on the truth and
the love we have for our Lord.

Remember in the Hebrew is *zakak*, which means to mark, to
think on, to burn incense. What a beautiful picture this is! We offer
a sacrifice of fragrance to the Most High God with the simple act of
remembering. Our prayers are a fragrance, our lives are a fragrance, and our times of remembering are a sweet sacrifice of fragrance to the throne of God.

As a couple, our prayer and purpose is for God to reveal to us
how to creatively tie our children's heartstrings to His truth so that
they will remember and celebrate their journey of faith. We desire
to create *kairos* time (moments) instead of *chronos* time (minutes)
with our family.

In the following chapters we look at practical ways to live out
the grace of remembering. We'll walk you through specific ideas
and practices that we've created for our family. The way you live
out celebrations in your house, or the way you create *kairos*
moments may be totally different from ours. You may come up with
new celebrations that you want to start, and we encourage that.

What's important to remember is that once you're convinced that
God wants you to create places of remembrance for your children,
then He will show you specifically how to do that. As our friend
Phyllis says, "If you know the *why*, God will show you the *how*."

❀ What do I remember about God as a child?

✿ What would I like my children to remember about God?

❀ How has unthankfulness in my own heart turned me away from God's goodness?

❀ What circumstances or attitudes keep me from being thankful?

Father God, teach me the grace of remembering. Teach me to sit at Your feet and to reflect on the majesty of Your work in my life. Teach me to cultivate the time in those moments to sit with my children and to lead them in the sacrament of remembering and the beauty of remembering. May I model a heart of gratitude to my children. I present these children to You, Father, and pray that I will not lose this generation or generations to come because I have ceased to sit at Your feet and humbly remember who You are.

5

The Joshua Basket

"We need only to remember the festivals and remembrances instituted by God to understand that 'sameness,' in the opinion of the Almighty can be a valuable anchor for the soul."
—Richard Swenson, M.D.[1]

"Jesus, thank You for Mommy and Daddy and . . . and . . . thank You for Lauren's piano," exclaimed Khrystian as she threw her hands in the air in praise to God.

That day in 1996 we were all thanking God as we knelt around the new musical addition to our home—a piano for Lauren. For two years as a family we prayed for Lauren's request for a piano with no indication of an answer. Lauren believed God would bring her a piano even if the rest of us had our doubts at times. Then one day out of the blue, a Christian woman we did not know called us.

"I was wondering . . . um . . . if you'd like to have my piano," she explained rather timidly. "I've tried to sell my piano, but God hasn't allowed it. I prayed about it, and the Lord told me He wanted my piano to go to a special family that would love using this piano for Him. The next day at work a friend gave me your phone number. I'd love to give you this piano, if you'd like to have it."

In honor of the memorable day Lauren's piano arrived, we painted a piano on stone #45 in *The Joshua Basket* in our living room. *The Joshua Basket* is set up as a memorial to remind our family how our *Jehovah Jireh*, our Provider, meets us time and time again in our journey of faith.

We created this first *Celebration of Faith* in 1986 after God showed us the significance of Joshua 4:4-7, 21-24:

> So Joshua called together the twelve men he had appointed from the Israelites, one from each tribe, and said to them, "Go over before the ark of the LORD your God into the middle of the Jordan. Each of you is to take up a stone on his shoulder, according to the number of the tribes of the Israelites, to serve as a sign among you. In the future, when your children ask you, 'What do these stones mean?' tell them that the flow of the Jordan was cut off before the ark of the covenant of the LORD. When it crossed the Jordan, the waters of the Jordan were cut off. These stones are to be a memorial to the people of Israel forever. . . .
>
> He said to the Israelites, "In the future when your descendants ask their fathers, 'What do these stones mean?' tell them, 'Israel crossed the Jordan on dry ground.' For the LORD your God dried up the Jordan before you until you had crossed over. The LORD your God did to the Jordan just what he had done to the Red Sea when he dried it up before us until we had crossed over. He did this so that all the peoples of the earth might know that the hand of the LORD is powerful and so that you might always fear the LORD your God.

God asked each tribe of the Israelites to take up stones and He instructed them, "These stones will be for your children. When they ask, 'Who is your God?' you will tell them." This passage is so powerful because it specifically tells us the stones were a monument of remembrance *for the children.*

God led Lisa to this Joshua passage when we were new to San Antonio and she was working through a depression after our first miscarriage. One day she tearfully prayed, "God, seal my heart with remembering Your goodness. Even in my pain, let Your goodness flow through me to my children." The Lord reassured her heart, "There is grace enough. Look to me."

God showed Lisa in the midst of her emptiness the hope-filled words of Joshua 4. Immediately, Lisa gathered our children and read them the passage, sharing of her idea for a remembrance basket. Our little ones clapped and exclaimed, "Oh yes, Mommy. This will be fun!" Lisa packed the kids in a stroller and headed to a nearby pond in a park to pick out the most beautiful, smooth stones she could find.

She placed the stones in a wicker basket and on the handle tied a tag with the name, *The Joshua Basket*. This celebration symbol still proudly sits in our living room with more than a decade of God-inspired memories. Stone by stone, we literally build a testimony of God's faithfulness in our lives.

It's encouraging to look in the Bible and see that the Lord Himself set aside stones of remembrance:

The stone Satan tempted Jesus to turn to bread.
The stone Jesus told the Pharisees to throw if they had no sin.
The stone used to teach the parents of God's good gifts to them.
The stone that was rolled in front of the tomb to seal
　　Christ's death.
The same stone rolled away three days later to crown
　　Christ's life.

Because we want our children regularly to see God's goodness and remember His faithfulness, we write our family prayer requests and date and number them in a journal that we keep inside our *Joshua Basket*. When God answers our prayers, we take a permanent marker and number a stone to match the answer to prayer.

Sometimes the kids empty the basket on the living room floor exclaiming, "Tell us about stone #19 or stone #35! Tell us again how God heard us and answered us." When guests come to our home, they soon notice and ask about *The Joshua Basket*. The children eagerly tell our guests all about Joshua 4 and God's faithfulness to us over the years.

On vacations we look for special stones to mark God's goodness and answers to prayer. On Thanksgiving we enjoy a special time of pulling out *The Joshua Basket* and remembering all of God's answers to our prayers for the year. It's also a great time to make a video or tape recording of the children telling their stories of the year's answered prayers.

What monument of remembrances does your family have? Creating your own *Joshua Basket* is a tremendous way to celebrate God's faithfulness to your family day by day, year after year. *The Joshua Basket* is our own Wilson family monument to *Jehovah Jireh*— our great Provider!

And, stone #45 with the hand-painted piano is always one of our favorite Joshua stones. To thank the sweet woman for Lauren's piano, we invited her to our home and presented her with her own *Joshua Basket*. Only *Jehovah Jireh* could stop the waters of the Jordan River and only *Jehovah Jireh* could deliver a free piano to a little girl who believes in miracles.

personal reflection

❧ What do I tell my children when they ask me about God?
❧ What are some ways God has specifically answered our family's prayers?
❧ How can we begin to record God's faithfulness to us over the years?

personal prayer

Father, our family offers up this tiny basket of stones as a monument for Your glory—The Rock of Ages! May we continually collect stones—as we walk through the wilderness of life, may we use the small dusty stones to remember our trials and Your daily provision. As we walk through the valleys, may we use the big stones that You placed by the rivers for us to rest upon and renew our strength and drink of Your goodness.

Your own memorial stones are a monument of glory here on earth. We revel in Your majesty! We offer up our sacrifice of praise to You, as living stones in Your building the body of Christ. You will present us with a white stone in heaven with our new names written on it. We will kneel before You, our Savior, Redeemer, Creator, and Chief Cornerstone! Amen.

tools for creating your own celebration

Purchase a complete *Joshua Basket,* including a *Joshua Journal*, at your local Christian bookstore or from Cook Communications (see page 223 for more information).
To assemble your own *Joshua Basket*, you'll need:
  Small to medium-sized stones
  Decorative basket
  Notebook or journal
  Permanent marker

6

Heart Birthdays

> "You have made known to me the path of life;
> you will fill me with joy in your presence,
> with eternal pleasures at your right hand."
> —*Psalm 16:11*

Three-year-old Lauren sat quietly on Lisa's lap listening to her mom explain the Easter story and how Jesus died but came back to life. Abruptly Lauren bopped her blonde pigtails around and looked seriously into Lisa's eyes.

"Mommy," Lauren sighed. "The sin in my heart hurts!" Lisa gently stroked Lauren's cheek and replied, "Well, sweetheart, would you like it to stop hurting?"

"Yes, Mommy!" Lauren quickly exclaimed. Taking a deep breath, Lisa prayed aloud for God to reveal Himself to Lauren and led her to invite Christ into her life. Still snuggled on Lisa's lap, Lauren finished the prayer herself and immediately looked up into her mom's eyes.

"Mommy! My heart doesn't hurt anymore!" This was an eternal moment where our little girl met God, and He came into her heart to live forever. Even at her young age, Lauren understood that sin hurts our heart and disappoints God.

We called that memorable day in 1987 Lauren's *Heart Birthday*, and we began to celebrate each child's special day of entering into a personal relationship with Jesus. We want our children to know that it's just as important to celebrate their heart birthdays—when they enter God's family—as it is to celebrate their physical birthdays when they came into our family. In a little frame in our living room, we've placed the words *Heart Birthday* and the date of each child's spiritual birthday.

To commemorate a *Heart Birthday*, each child gets a heart-shaped cake with candles on it for the number of years he or she has known Christ. We place a string of white miniature Christmas lights around the cake (we keep the lights handy all year long for these celebrations).

The child whose *Heart Birthday* we're celebrating then gives a simple testimony about how he or she came to faith in Jesus. Next, Randy speaks a blessing over the child, and we all sing "Happy Birthday" as the birthday honoree blows out the candles.

Celebrate the heart of your child! Bake a cake, speak the Scriptures, and enjoy. You can also start a collection of a heart-themed gifts on each child's spiritual birthday: heart-shaped boxes, biographies of great saints in history, heart-shaped jewelry, or whatever God leads you to give. Yearly celebrating each child's life-changing decision helps the child remember the eternal significance of a personal commitment to God.

personal reflection

✿ Why is it important to remember when we receive God's gift of salvation?

✿ What does God say in His Word about the joy of knowing Him?

✿ How can I help my children celebrate their *Heart Birthday*?

✿ What collection of gifts can I start for my children to celebrate their spiritual birthdays?

personal prayer

Father God, place a hedge of protection around the hearts of my children. I pray them into Your kingdom. I ask that You would make their hearts like well-watered gardens whose waters do not fail. May You protect them, cover them, nurture them, and guard them from the wickedness and distractions of this world as they seek You.

Lord, help me as a parent do everything I can to place a covering of wise protection and guidance over each child's heart. When my children place their trust in You, we want to celebrate with the angels that they are truly Yours. Thank You for hearing my prayer, gracious Lord. Amen.

tools for creating your own celebration

Heart-shaped cake
Birthday candles
Set of miniature lights
Heart-themed gift of your choosing

7

The Proverbs Notebook

> **❝**The fear of the Lord is the beginning
> of knowledge, but fools despise wisdom
> and discipline.
> Listen, my son, to your father's instruction
> and do not forsake your mother's teaching.**❞**
> —*Proverbs 1:7-8*

At the top of her notebook, eleven-year-old Lauren wrote Proverbs 22:12: "The eyes of the LORD keep watch over knowledge, but he frustrates the words of the unfaithful." Under this verse she drew two pictures. One drawing shows Jesus in a house standing watch over our family. The other drawing caught us a bit off guard, and we asked Lauren to explain it.

"That's the President with his daughter beside him in front of a TV camera," Lauren explained. "That's the huge hand of God covering the President's mouth." Five years later we are still amazed at our daughter's vivid interpretation of this verse in Proverbs—God steps in to "frustrate the words of the unfaithful."

We love the Book of Proverbs, and we wanted to introduce our little ones to this ancient book of wisdom. Before our children could even read, we picked up some blank journals and created a

Proverbs Notebook for each child. At the top of a notebook page we would write out a verse from Proverbs, and the child would draw his or her own pictures describing the principle of the verse.

Because most of the proverbs are divided into two parts—the good does this and the bad does that—they are easy for children to understand. Our kids love drawing these pictures, and as they've grown older, their pictures depict more details of Solomon's stories. As our children ponder the verses and then draw their interpretations of the verses, God's Word is etched upon their hearts and minds.

We are constantly awed by our children's insights as they draw pictures of the truth. When our sons and daughters leave home, they'll take a stack of *Proverbs Notebooks* with them to remember the hours of learning the Scriptures together at the kitchen table.

Begin today with this fun way to teach your children God's Word. Year after year, your children will love creating their own "coloring book" of the Bible.

Children love to show their *Proverbs Notebooks* to family, friends, and houseguests. As your children explain their drawings, you can tell them your own childhood stories or how a particular verse in Proverbs helped you. Grandparents enjoy this activity too. What a natural way to pass along your family heritage!

personal reflection

❈ What do I remember most about the Book of Proverbs?
❈ What practical lessons for everyday living can I teach my children through Proverbs?
❈ How can I teach God's wisdom and understanding to my children?

personal prayer

Lord, I pray that my children would grow to love the Book of Proverbs. I ask that they would seek wisdom and would sit at wisdom's feet. I pray that they would listen to wisdom as she rebukes them, calls them, and counsels them. As my children grow into adulthood, may they enjoy the fruit of loving wisdom and seeking wisdom with all their hearts, souls, and minds. May they not listen to folly, but stand as wisdom seekers all the days of their lives. Amen.

tools for creating your own celebration

The Book of Proverbs
Blank journal or notebook
Crayons, colored pencils, or markers

8

The Scripture Recital

> **"My heart is stirred by a noble theme
> as I recite my verses for the king;
> my tongue is the pen of a skillful writer."**
> —*Psalm 45:1*

After our second miscarriage, our family grieved the loss tremendously. We prayed together that God would give us another baby, and according to the doctor, literally within days Lisa conceived again. One morning after Logan was born, we gasped as we found ten-year-old Colten snuggled inside his baby brother's crib reading from the Bible.

As Logan lay there cooing and eyeing his big brother, Colten gently instructed his newborn brother, "Logan, ya gotta know the Word. Ya gotta know the Word of God."

Teaching our children to *know* the Word of God is the burning passion of our hearts. Even before our children were born, we desired to consistently present His Word to them. As 2 Timothy 3:15 tells us about a little boy, "From infancy you have known the holy Scriptures, which are able to make you wise for salvation through faith in Christ Jesus."

As Lisa carried each baby in her womb, we would read Bible passages out loud and sing praise songs and hymns to bless our child. In the moments after our first child, Lauren, was born, Randy spoke the Scriptures to her as we named her. When we brought her home, Randy read the Scriptures to her daily. When Lauren moved to her own room, he tape recorded large passages of the Word for her to go to sleep by.

We've repeated this with each of our other five children. We also place above each child's bed a paper banner with Scriptures written on it. As our children read the Scripture banner every night before falling asleep, they quickly memorize the verses.

British art critic and writer John Ruskin recalls the importance of learning the Bible at the knee of his Scottish Presbyterian mother.

> My mother's influence in molding my character was conspicuous. She forced me to learn daily long chapters of the Bible by heart. To that disciplined, patient, accurate resolve, I owe not only much of my general power for taking pains, but the best part of my taste for literature.[1]

As the children have grown older, we've chosen large passages of Scripture for them to memorize such as Psalms 103 and 119 and Colossians 3. We've also helped them learn the Hebrew names of God (see chapter nine) and Scriptures stating who they are in Christ (see chapter fifteen).

We've attended a number of recitals—drama, piano, oral interpretation—so we thought, *Why not a Scripture recital?* When our children finish memorizing several portions of Scripture, we invite family and friends to our home for a formal *Scripture Recital* sharing in the beauty of our children speaking God's Word.

For as Deuteronomy 4:9 reminds us, "Only give heed to yourself and keep your soul diligently, lest you forget the things which your eyes have seen, and lest they depart from your heart all the days of your life; but make them known to your sons and your grandsons" (NASB).

line upon line

Because we home school, during the school year our kids spend an hour to an hour-and-a-half a day in devotions and memorizing and reciting Bible verses. It's so encouraging to listen as our children talk about what a particular Scripture verse means to them *line upon line*.

Isaiah 28:9-10 directs us, "'To whom would He teach knowledge? And to whom would He interpret the message? . . . For He says, order on order, order on order, Line on line, line on line, a little here, a little there'" (NASB). Line upon line we are diligently to teach our sons and daughters the Scriptures. If we open their spirits to God, He will open their minds to everything else.

Many a day our littlest ones will stand in front of the fireplace with tiny books and Bibles in their hands, imitating their older siblings. Even though they have no idea what they're saying, our toddlers pretend that they're memorizing Scripture.

If we are not exalting the Scriptures and God in our home, what are we exalting? The greatest thing we can give our children is God's Word—period. If our children leave home turning to His Word, we've done our job. We will have taught them to follow the words of Job 23:12, "I have not departed from the command of His lips; I have treasured the words of His mouth more than my necessary food" (NASB).

John Randolph, a distinguished American statesman, once explained what preserved him from indulging in the many seductions of infidelity he faced because of his position:

> I believe I should have been swept away by the flood of French infidelity, if it had not been for one thing, the remembrance of the time, when my sainted mother used to make me kneel by her side, taking my little hands folded in hers, and caused me to repeat the Lord's Prayer.[2]

What are you doing to preserve your children?

To begin a *Scripture Recital* celebration, choose passages of Scripture meaningful in your family for your children to memorize. You might also print these passages on large banners and hang them where you'll see and review them often. If memorizing Scripture is new to your children, start modestly with verses or sections the children are already familiar with.

personal reflection

❀ What importance do I place on God's Word in my life?
❀ How am I exalting the Scriptures in my home?
❀ How can I teach my children to treasure God's precepts?

personal prayer

Father God, I pray that Your Scripture would be exalted in our home, that above all, my children's hearts and minds would be filled with the sacred power of Your Word, the very Word of Life. I pray that my children would come to love the Scriptures, know the Scriptures, remember the Scriptures, exalt the Scriptures, and live the Scriptures as they hide them in their hearts. May Your Word preserve them from evil all the days of their lives. Thank You for the power of Your mighty Word. Empower me to do all I can to set aside time to teach my children Your Holy Word.

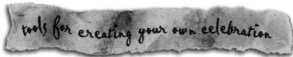

tools for creating your own celebration

Bible
Paper banners or signs
Colored markers or pens
Tape recorder and blank cassette tapes

9

The Names of God

> **❝** I will cause Thy name to be remembered in all generations; Therefore the peoples will give Thee thanks forever and ever. **❞**
> —*Psalm 45:17,* NASB

During Colten's sixth-grade year, he produced an amazing oral interpretation of the life and times of George Washington. Colten asked to visit a public school and present his research on George Washington, emphasizing this American President's biblical faith. We assured our son that his boldness would truly honor God.

The week of Colten's presentation we needed to pick up his patriotic costume at a local shop, but our checking account was near zero. We knew we could not change the date with the school, so without a word to Colten, we began to pray for God to show up with the needed cash.

As Lisa drove Colten to the shop, she silently prayed for the Lord to make a way for Colten to rent his costume and give his presentation. As Colten and Lisa entered the store, they noticed an older woman in the back. Lisa struck up a conversation and the woman asked why Colten wanted to rent replica clothing of George Washington.

Upon hearing Colten's purpose, the woman said, "You know what? Why don't you just take the outfit. I really like what you're doing. Just take the costume for free. As matter of fact, any time you want to use the costume again, just tell people about our shop, and there'll be no charge for you."

God is the God of the George Washington costume, and He showed up in this tiny costume shop in Colorado Springs. This owner just happened to be there that day, and she had no idea that Lisa walked in not knowing how to pay the rental fee.

Tears ran down Lisa's cheeks as she and Colten walked out to the parking lot. "Honey, God is God, and He provided from the heavens for us today," Lisa explained to our son. "*Jehovah Jireh*, our Provider, came down to this little shop and provided this costume for you because you are going to honor Him and tell the true story of George Washington."

On the drive home, Lisa exuberantly explained about our lack of funds and how Mom and Dad prayed asking in faith for God's timely provisions. That memorial event (#76 in our *Joshua Basket*) reassured Colten that *Jehovah Adonai* literally directed a way for him to stand in front of other school children to magnify the Lord in the life of this honorable man in history.

understanding God's character

As a testimony to our children, we constantly try to teach them the Hebrew names of God. We introduce our children to the very character of God through His names as they pray and seek Him. For example, when they are feeling scared, we can pray to *Jehovah Shamah* for His presence, or when they are sick we call upon *Jehovah Rapha*, the God who heals.

We wrote the Hebrew names on posters and placed them on our walls. You can write the names on 3 x 5 cards to place in a basket on your table. After a meal, or as part of your family time, have each child pick one to review; the family can learn the Scripture to go with it.

Psalm 143:11 declares: "Quicken me, O LORD, for thy name's sake: for thy righteousness' sake, bring my soul out of trouble" (KJV). For His name's sake, He can bring us out of trouble. We find strength, comfort, hope, and victory in life when we know and call upon the supreme names of God.

To help us celebrate the names of God, our dear friend and mentor Bruce McDonald has allowed us to reprint his study list of Hebrew names. Helping your children know the powerful names of God invites them to call upon God in any situation and watch Him work mightily on their behalf. After all, our *Elohim* is a God of details who knows exactly when to surprise a young boy with a free costume.

the names of God

JEHOVAH—Lord God, Self-Existent One Who Reveals
    Himself
JEHOVAH JIREH—The Lord Provides
1 John 4:9; Psalm 116:5,8,16,17
JEHOVAH NISSE—The Lord Our Banner
1 Chronicles 29:11-13
JEHOVAH ROPHI—The Lord Heals
Isaiah 53:4-5; Acts 4:12; 1 Peter 2:24
JEHOVAH ROHI—The Lord My Shepherd
Psalm 23:3-5; John 14:26, 16:13
JEHOVAH SHALOM—The Lord Our Peace
Psalm 29:1; Isaiah 9:6; Romans 8:31-35
JEHOVAH T'SIDKENU—The Lord Our Righteousness
Psalm 48:10; Psalm 119:137; Daniel 9:14; Hosea 14:9;
    Romans 10:4; 1 Corinthians 1:30
JEHOVAH SHAMMAH—The Lord Is Present
Psalm 139:7-8; Isaiah 66:1-2; Hebrews 13:5-6
JEHOVAH M'KADDESH—The Lord Who Sanctifies
Isaiah 57:15; 1 John 1:5; Revelation 4:8, 15:4
JEHOVAH SABAOTH—The Lord of Hosts
1 Samuel 1:3; Isaiah 6:3

ADONAI—Lord, Owner Master, Supreme Authority
Genesis 15:2
ELOHIM—God, Strong, Faithful One Who Keeps His
   Covenant
Genesis 1:1; Exodus 34:6

Throughout the Bible we find references to God's matchless
name. Here are a few verses to encourage your family to lift up the
glorious name of *Jehovah Sabaoth*:

But let all who take refuge in you be glad; let them ever
   sing for joy. Spread your protection over them, that
   those who love your name may rejoice in you (Ps.
   5:11).
O LORD, our Lord, how majestic is your name in all the
   earth! You have set your glory above the heavens (Ps.
   8:1).
Those who know your name will trust in you, for you,
   LORD, have never forsaken those who seek you (Ps.
   9:10).
Through you we push back our enemies; through your
   name we trample our foes (Ps. 44:5).
I will sacrifice a freewill offering to you; I will praise your
   name, O LORD, for it is good (Ps. 54:6).
Teach me your way, O LORD, and I will walk in your truth;
   give me an undivided heart, that I may fear your name
   (Ps. 86:11).
I will praise you, O Lord my God, with all my heart; I will
   glorify your name forever (Ps. 86:12).
In the night I remember your name, O LORD, and I will
   keep your law (Ps. 119:55).
Your name, O LORD, endures forever, your renown, O
   LORD, through all generations (Ps. 135:13).
I will exalt you, my God the King; I will praise your name
   for ever and ever (Ps. 145:1).
No one is like you, O LORD; you are great, and your name
   is mighty in power (Jer. 10:6).

This is how you should pray: "Our Father in heaven, hallowed be your name" (Matt. 6:9).

Who will not fear you, O Lord, and bring glory to your name? For you alone are holy. All nations will come and worship before you, for your righteous acts have been revealed (Rev. 15:4).

❀ How can calling upon God's many names strengthen my faith?

❀ What one character of God do I need to rest in today?

❀ How can I begin to teach my children the names of their God?

Adonai, I exalt You in the beauty and the power of all of Your names. Thank You that You chose to reveal Yourself in so many ways to Your people in the Scriptures. Thank You that we can intimately know You, *Jehovah Nisse*, through knowing the beautiful names that You have given us.

Elohim, I pray that my family would speak Your names with reverence, and that we would diligently learn Your names and claim them as a hedge of protection around us. May we follow You, *Jehovah Rohi*, our Great Shepherd, and rest in Your peace, *Jehovah Shalom*. Amen.

10

Personal Belief Statement

> ❝Yet to all who received him, to those who believed in his name, he gave the right to become children of God.❞
> —*John 1:12*

The sun pokes through the lace curtains in our kitchen as Lisa lights a candle on the kitchen table and the kids finish their home-made cinnamon rolls. Every morning after breakfast, we read and recite Scriptures together. When God spoke His Word, He ordered chaos and created truth. When Satan tempted Jesus in the wilderness, Jesus responded with "it is written."

For centuries, the church has publicly declared its beliefs in God's Word through such written statements as the Apostle's Creed, the Nicene Creed, and the Westminster Confession of Faith. As author John Bevere writes, "Doctrine does not establish our relationship with God; it only defines it!"[1]

One way we define our faith is by occasionally reading aloud the affirmation of faith taken from Neil Anderson's book *The Bondage Breaker*. Our older children have added these powerful truths to their Scripture memorization.

Perhaps before attending church or even on the drive to or from a worship service, you can take turns reading aloud a paragraph from this rich statement. Or you may want to review the affirmations at a special family gathering or a *Scripture Recital*.

I recognize that there is only one true and living God (Exodus 20:2-3) who exists as the Father, Son, and Holy Spirit, and that He is worthy of all honor, praise, and worship as the Creator, Sustainer, and Beginning and End of all things (Revelation 1:8, 4:11; 5:9-10; Isaiah 43:1,7,21).

I recognize Jesus Christ as the Messiah, the Word who became flesh and dwelt among us (John 1:1,14). I believe that He came to destroy the works of Satan (1 John 3:8), that He disarmed the rulers and authorities and made a public display of them, having triumphed over them (Colossians 2:15).

I believe that God has proven His love for me, because when I was still a sinner Christ died for me (Romans 5:8). I believe that He delivered me from the domain of darkness and transferred me to His kingdom, and in Him I have redemption, the forgiveness of sins (Colossians 1:13-14).

I believe that I am now a child of God (1 John 3:1-3), and that I am seated with Christ in the heavenlies (Ephesians 2:6). I believe that I was saved by the grace of God through faith, that it was a gift and not the result of any works on my part (Ephesians 2:8).

I choose to be strong in the Lord and in the strength of His might (Ephesians 6:10). I put no confidence in the flesh (Philippians 3:3), for the weapons of warfare are not of the flesh (2 Corinthians 10:4). I put on the whole armor of God (Ephesians 6:10-17), and I resolve to stand firm in my faith and resist the evil one.

I believe that Jesus has all authority in heaven and on earth (Matthew 28:18), and that He is the head over all rule and authority (Colossians 2:10). I believe that Satan and his demons are subject to me in Christ because I am a member of Christ's body (Ephesians 1:19-23). I therefore obey the command to resist the devil (James 4:7), and command him in the name of Christ to leave my presence.

I believe that apart from Christ I can do nothing (John 15:5), so I declare my dependence on Him. I choose to abide in Christ in order to bear much fruit and glorify the Lord (John 15:8). I announce to Satan that Jesus is my Lord (1 Corinthians 12:3), and I reject any counterfeit gifts or works of Satan in my life.

I believe that the truth will set me free (John 8:32), and that walking in the light is the only path of fellowship (1 John 1:7). Therefore, I stand against Satan's deception by taking every thought captive in obedience to Christ (2 Corinthians 10:5). I declare that the Bible is the only authoritative standard (2 Timothy 3:15-17). I choose to speak the truth in love (Ephesians 4:15).

I choose to present my body as an instrument of righteousness, a living and holy sacrifice, and I renew my mind by the living Word of God in order that I may prove that the will of God is good, acceptable, and perfect (Romans 6:13; 12:1-2).

I ask my heavenly Father to fill me with His Holy Spirit (Ephesians 5:18), to lead me into all truth (John 16:13), and empower my life so that I may live above sin and not carry out the desires of the flesh (Galatians 5:16). I crucify the flesh (Galatians 5:24) and choose to walk by the Spirit.

I renounce all selfish goals and choose the ultimate goal of love (1 Timothy 1:5). I choose to obey the greatest commandment, to love the Lord my God with all my heart, soul, and mind, and to love my neighbor as myself (Matthew 22:37-39).[2]

personal reflection

✤ Do I really understand the biblical foundations of my faith?

✤ How can I use historic belief statements to refresh my own beliefs?

✤ How can I teach my children the rich truths of Christianity?

personal prayer

Lord, I thank You for Your doctrine and the rock-solid foundations of Scripture. May I be diligent in presenting these pillars of the Word of God to my children to anchor their souls. Guard the seeds of truth planted in my children's hearts by these affirmations of faith. Cultivate the richness of these declarations in their minds so that my children would never waver in faith or be led astray by false teaching. Ground each of us in the knowledge of You and Your Holy Word. Amen.

tools for creating your own celebration

Copies of creeds or doctrines to read and memorize

11

Wisdom Basket

66 My son, if you accept my words and store up my commands within you, turning your ear to wisdom and applying your heart to understanding, and if you call out for insight and cry aloud for understanding, and if you look for it as for silver and search for it as for hidden treasure, then you will understand the fear of the LORD and find the knowledge of God. For the LORD gives wisdom, and from his mouth come knowledge and understanding. 99
—*Proverbs 2:1-6*

After dinner we invited our guests, a young married couple, to relax in our living room with us. Our children eagerly reached into our *Wisdom Basket*—a small basket filled with laminated slips of paper that sits in our living room. Each slip lists a question for our children to ask of Christians who visit our home.

This particular night, the first question was: What is your first memory of knowing that God is real? Our whole family still remembers the wife tearfully recounting a tragic car accident that nearly killed her and forced her into a year of intense rehabilitation.

Through her trauma, this young woman who casually knew God grew to love the God of miracles who spared her life.

Our children love these fascinating moments with our guests. We designed the *Wisdom Basket* to help teach our children to ask wise and meaningful questions. The ability to ask questions and listen to someone's response is one of the greatest gifts we can pass on to our children.

Wise questions set a tone of honor. Our children learn humility by asking a question and quietly learning from our guests' response. Asking skilled questions is a lifelong skill that will bring great reward to our children's hearts. Jesus was a master at asking wise questions. Questions open our hearts and display value and significance.

Here are sample questions from our *Wisdom Basket*. Take a few minutes with your children to write some intriguing questions of your own. Your *Wisdom Basket* will become a fun family tradition for years to come.

What story in the Bible makes you laugh?

When you get to heaven, what is the first thing you want to say to God?

What is the hardest thing for you to understand about God?

What is your first memory of knowing that God is real?

Who has influenced your life the most?

Who is your favorite historical person who has influenced you?

Who is your favorite author and what is your favorite book?

When did you ask Christ into your heart to be your Savior?

When you read about Jesus, what do you love about Him the most?

What has been your greatest joy?

Did you have a favorite teacher? Tell us about him or her.

As a child, what did you want to be when you grew up?

What is your spiritual gift? God-given natural gifts?

How and when do you have a devotional time?
If you could live any part of your life over again, what part
would that be and why?
What Bible character would you like to talk to the most?
What has been the biggest answer to prayer in your life?
What is your favorite hymn/praise song?

personal reflection

❦ How can asking questions teach my children about life,
about God?

❦ How can I teach the skills of observation and discussion to
my kids?

❦ When can we sit down as a family and come up with our
own intriguing questions?

personal prayer

Lord, You tell us in Proverbs to gain wisdom, and above all,
to gain understanding. I pray that my children would be
great question-askers, that asking wise questions would be
a natural part of their lives so that they could walk into
anyone's world and learn from them and honor them.
Thank You that Jesus was the perfect model of asking
poignant questions and getting to the heart of the matter.

May my children learn discernment and understanding
as Your Spirit leads them in conversations with others.
Father, help my children truly listen to the older people in
their lives who can give them a deeper understanding of
who You are. Develop a humble spirit in each child and a
desire to constantly seek Your face through the lives of
cherished saints who enter our home. Amen.

tools for creating your own celebration

Small basket or decorative box
Handwritten or typed list of questions
Clear adhesive plastic for lamination (or take sheet of
    questions to a printing service)
Scissors

12

Mom and Dad's Book of Treasures

> **"** How we remember, what we remember, and why we remember form the most personal map of our individuality. **"**
> —*Christina Baldwin*[1]

One evening before dinner Randy sat at the dining room table visibly troubled. Choking back tears, Randy shared about God's faithfulness in our passages of pain. Just coming out of three years of spiritual assault on his reputation, Randy wanted our children to understand God's presence in our tough times and not just His presence when life seems contented.

That night we decided to create a scrapbook detailing bits and pieces of our family legacy, including passages of joy and passages of pain. We wanted our children to see where they've come from and where they are going as God is writing His story in our family. We've titled our scrapbook *Mom and Dad's Book of Treasures.*

Is God still faithful when we encounter trials? Can we trust Him if we can't see or hear Him? God's hand is over both our physical genetics as well as our spiritual genetics. How much of your spiritual journey have you shared with your children? How are you keeping a record of God's hand in your lives for the generations to come? Our recorded journey as a family is divided into the following sections:

1. Letters and pictures from our friends and mentors who've spurred us on in our faith.
2. Favorite Bible studies and Bible teachers.
3. Favorite hymns and praise songs.
4. Passages of pain with Scripture and a testimony of how God led us through the difficulties.
5. Passages of joy where God touched us deeply.
6. Favorite quotes and Bible verses.

Mom and Dad's Book of Treasures is a memory book of God Himself touching each generation in our family. Our personal history is truly His Story. You can adapt this celebration to your family interests and schedule. Every few months we sit down as a family and update our book with new photos, stories, and verses. The kids love to arrange the entries onto the pages. (Don't worry about the perfect layout—you are not competing in a creative arts contest!) Make some popcorn and plop down in the family room for a time of reminiscing and creative fun.

personal reflection

✻ Who are the special friends and mentors to our family?
✦ What are my family's favorite Bible verses and songs?
✤ How can we preserve treasures of our spiritual journey?

personal prayer

Father, help me leave a legacy of hidden treasures for my children in this book of memories. When the children read the spiritual journey of our lives, may they see not only the joys, but also the pains and the twists in our paths. Above all, open my children's eyes to Your steady faithfulness and Your enduring love even in our darkest times. Lord, may my children preserve the rich legacy in their own lives and pass it on to their children. Our God Most High, may You be high and lifted up in the personal journeys of our heart and spirit.

tools for creating your own celebration

Scrapbook or photo album with room for added pages
Collection of your favorite photos, stories, and Scriptures
Photo corners, glue, markers, scissors

13

Celebrate the Sabbath

❝ Come, let us bow down in worship,
let us kneel before the LORD our Maker;
for he is our God and we are the people
of his pasture, the flock under his care. **❞**
—Psalm 95:6-7

We sat with arms crossed, separated by a thick cloud of tension. We were inches away from each other in the church pew, but our hearts were miles apart. Another Sunday morning of struggling with dressing and loading up the kids had shoved us into overload. Even a 7-Eleven vanilla coffee couldn't soothe our rumpled spirits.

When we were first married, it seemed our fights would start on Friday night and end on Sunday night. One day we looked at each other and said, "This is ridiculous! You realize there is a plan here to assault our marriage, and it's on the weekend, right when we're going into the Sabbath and should be enjoying each other and enjoying God."

Perhaps you can relate to the stress of preparing your family for worship services. When our kids were little, we would literally begin on Friday night finding the shoes, tights, and bows, and ironing suits and dresses. On Saturday night we'd spread out diaper bags and all the kids' clothes on the couch, and on Sunday morning form an assembly line to dress each child. It's no wonder we were on edge by the time we arrived at church with our energetic little ones!

It didn't take us long to realize we needed to change our worship focus. One day we read 2 Chronicles 20:13 describing entire families worshiping together before God: *"All the men of Judah, with their wives and children and little ones, stood there before the LORD."* God impressed this verse on our hearts, and we began to teach our children what it means to listen and cultivate a calm spirit before God. Satan majors in chaos and disorder, so we also began to pray for God's protection over our Sabbath time.

It's common for churches to set aside a time for children's church during a worship service, but rarely do you see children sit with their parents during corporate worship. Most children are not included in a regular worship service, so they do not know what it means to sit and worship God with a quiet spirit. After the birth of our first child, we decided to include our children in corporate worship services.

Where else would they *see* Mom and Dad worship? The Lord showed us Job 32:8, "But it is *the spirit in a man*, the breath of the Almighty, that *gives him understanding.*" *Our children can understand in their spirits what they can't comprehend in their minds.* Even if we do not know calculus, we can know God!

"It is perfectly clear that a child before he can speak is susceptible of moral training. The conscience, or moral sense, may…be developed soon after, if not before, the child has spent his first birthday," writes the author of *Female Piety*.[1]

To prepare our children for Sunday worship with us, we decided to nurture a quiet spirit in our children throughout the week. For each baby and toddler, Lisa took a soft baby blanket and with fabric paint wrote "Worship the Lord" and the child's name at the top. Every day during the week Lisa would lay the little ones on their own *Worship Blanket* or snuggle them under the blanket on her lap. That time with their special blanket represented a time for quietness.

While the children rested with their *Worship Blankets*, Lisa would read from the Bible or play worship tapes. We were creating a pattern for quietness and worship. On Sundays we took the *Worship Blankets* to church, so the children realized that worship does not start at church but at home.

Lisa also created a *Sabbath Bag* for our younger kids by writing their names with fabric paint on small canvas bags. We place a small Bible, a quiet toy, crayons and note pad, and the *Worship Blanket* in each bag. The little ones are not allowed to play with their *Sabbath Bag* except during Sunday worship services. A *Sabbath Bag* helps them to focus on God when they enter His house for worship.

To celebrate the Sabbath, we begin to gather our clothes and *Sabbath Bags* on Friday nights. We try to set aside Saturday nights for just our family and limit social activities. Throughout the week, we also listen to praise and worship tapes in the evenings especially as our children settle into bed. On Sunday mornings as we get ready for church, we continue to calm our spirits through uplifting music.

To help set a tone of quietness and worship for Sundays, Randy has set up these family guidelines:

Dedicate the weekend to the Lord.

Evaluate what works for the ages of the children. What are their physical and emotional needs as we cultivate quietness in their hearts?

Eliminate extra stress and distractions by planning ahead.

Concentrate on the goal of Christ-centered worship through prayer and worship music throughout the home.

Meditate on the Word and prepare the children through reading Scriptures.

Instead of dragging into church with your kids wound up and your spirit frazzled, think about gradually throughout the week preparing your family's hearts and minds to celebrate the Sabbath. As you seek God together as a family, remember that your *Jehovah*

Shalom longs to soothe your souls and lead you "beside quiet waters" (Ps. 23:2).

personal reflection

❋ How comfortable are my children with stillness or silence?
❋ What is one thing I can do this week to nurture a quiet
     spirit in my children?
❋ How can I prepare ahead for an easier, calmer transition
     into the Sabbath?

personal prayer

Lord God, in this hectic, fast-paced world, help me gently
and purposefully cultivate the beauty of the Sabbath. Show
me how to prepare ahead of time and teach my children
the beauty of the day of rest. I pray the Enemy would gain
no footholds over our Sabbath celebrations. Through music
and meditation throughout the week, guide our hearts and
minds to exalt Your name. Calm our anxious thoughts and
restless spirits. Father, help my children experience the
Sabbath as a day set apart to worship You. Amen.

tools for creating your own celebration

Child's blanket
Fabric paint or marker
Canvas or cloth bag
Children's Bible and notebook
Instrumental music tapes, quiet toys, crayons, and
    coloring pad

14

The Secret Place

"" The saints of past centuries knew the
value of having quiet times with the Lord.
They retired to their prayer closet or to a
secluded hillside every day. . . . If you will
take time to make some 'quiet spaces' for
meditating, praying, and worshipping
God, you will find far more strength in
your spirit than you have now. ""
—*Lester Sumrall*[1]

Sometimes we wonder what the ushers think on Sunday mornings when we unload a menagerie of suckers, crumpled notes to God, and rocks in the offering plate. No matter what others think of the Wilson family offerings, we know that God is delighted in our children's gifts. And He delights in our children as they slip away to meet with Him alone in a room we call *The Secret Place*.

The Hebrew word for "secret place" is *sether*; a hiding place, a covering. The Bible tells us God covered David in the shadow of His wings (Ps. 36:7), and David declared, "You are my hiding place; you will protect me from trouble and surround me with songs of deliverance" (Ps. 32:7).

The Lord promises us in Isaiah 45:3, "I will give you the treasures of darkness, riches stored in secret places, so that you may know that I am the LORD, the God of Israel, who calls you by name." In Psalm 44: 20-21 He reassures us: "If we had forgotten the name of our God or spread out our hands to a foreign god, would not God have discovered it, since he knows the secrets of the heart?"

The author of *The Shelter of Each Other* reaffirms children's need for a secret place. "Children's needs are not necessarily what we assume. Children like coziness, adults nearby and safe places to hide out and watch activities. They like routines, predictability and familiar places. This gives them a sense of control. They like tree houses, alleys, and places under stairways. Oftentimes with children smaller is better because smaller means closer and more navigable. The spaces we construct for children and the spaces that we leave alone for them affect their mental health."[2]

With a small house and six kids, we decided to set aside a place in our home where our children could go to quiet their spirits and listen to God. We bought about twenty-five yards of muslin-type fabric and draped it in a corner of the basement, so the two sides create a tiny, square room. We fastened wood dowels to the wall and draped the fabric over these dowels.

Large tassels hang behind the drapes, and the kids can pull them closed. A sign hung on tassels in the front says, *The Secret Place*. With fabric paint we wrote the Hebrew names of God on the same material and lined the inside walls. Big pillows and a large soft cushion are spread on the floor for our kids to sit on.

To introduce this *Celebration of Faith* to our children, we kept them out of the basement as we set up the secret throne room. The mystery and suspense made this new celebration even more fun! Then before the kids could discover their surprise, they had to figure out a secret code we wrote based on Psalm 25:14 (NASB): "The secret of the LORD is for those who fear Him, and He will make them know His covenant."

The Secret Place is a refuge for our children to get away and listen to God and write what He's telling them at that moment. In a corner of this private room, the children keep their Bibles, pens, journals, and a flashlight. They have headphones and a tape player to listen to praise music. Our kids meet with God in *The Secret Place* much like Jesus talks about in Matthew 6:6: "When you pray, go into your room, close the door and pray to your Father, who is unseen. Then your Father, who sees what is done in secret, will reward you."

We've also turned a hinged, gold jewelry box into a *Secrets Treasure Chest*, where our children put their secrets to the Lord: personal letters to God or 3 x 5 cards with notes about Scriptures they have read. The children also slip their offerings to the Lord in an envelope to take to church—yes, even their favorite suckers and rocks.

* How do I calm my spirit to listen to God?
* How serious am I about meeting with God in my own secret place?
* Do I instill the habit of quietness in my children?
* What place can I set aside for my children to cultivate a quiet, still spirit that listens to God?

Father, I commit a secret place to You, a quiet place where my children can slow down and listen to Your Spirit in their lives. Guard this soothing place in our home from distractions and the Enemy's whispers. May my children reverence and adore You as they seek time with their holy God.

Thank You that You cover us under the shadow of Your wings and that You desire to reveal Yourself to us. Pour out Your water of life upon my children as they sit alone at Your feet. As my little ones ponder the Scriptures and talk to You in prayer in their place of sacred quietness, may Your Spirit breathe into them the path of righteousness for Your name's sake. Amen.

tools for creating your own celebration

Fabric and tassels
Dowels for hanging fabric
Fabric paint or permanent marker
Pillows and cushions
A treasure chest (jewelry chest or decorated cardboard box)

PART THREE

The Gift of Purpose

15
Who Am I?

> **"We don't see things as they are,
> we see them as we are."**
> —*Anais Nin*[1]

When Thomas Edison painstakingly worked on improving his first electric light bulb, the story goes that he handed the finished bulb to a young helper. The boy nervously carried it upstairs, step by step. At the last possible moment, the helper dropped the bulb—requiring the whole team to work another twenty-four hours to make a second bulb. When the new bulb was finished, Edison looked around, then handed it to the same boy.

The gesture most assuredly changed the boy's life. Edison knew that more than a bulb was at stake. His decision to trust the boy with this monumental invention said to the young man: "I believe in you. We all make mistakes, but you have a significant purpose to fulfill in life."

Knowing our personal significance and purpose is foundational to living life fully as God intends. Purpose gives us a mission and direction. Without purpose we wander aimlessly, conforming to whatever comes our way. Noah Webster's original 1828 dictionary defines "purpose" as "to intend; to design; to resolve; to determine on some end or subject to be accomplished."[2]

Purpose frees us to design a plan for our lives and our children's lives.

Purpose gives energy and fuels passion.

Purpose identifies boundaries.

Purpose streamlines goals and creates a vision, for "where
there is no vision, the people perish (Prov. 29:18, KJV).

Purpose exposes spiritual beauty as we see our lives
through God's eyes and heart.

Purpose celebrates the integrity of intent.

Purpose creates space for greater capacity in determination
and courage.

Purpose solidifies God's plan for us in our generation.

This section of the book shows you how to pass on the *Gift of Purpose* to your children. At the end of this chapter (pages 102-103), we've included our personal purpose statements. We encourage you to write your purpose statement as a parent. How do you want God to direct you as a parent? What is your mission for your family?

Then as you read the next several chapters, choose one or more of our *Celebrations of Faith* to incorporate in your family's life.

understanding each child's gifts

Jordan is our compassionate child with a merciful heart. One morning Khrystian came downstairs and said, "Mom, Jordan kept me up all night! She was crying." Jordan shuffled into the kitchen and laid her head on Lisa's lap and sobbed, "Mommy, I had the most horrible dream. It was so bad, I can't even tell you."

"Sweetheart, it's okay. You can tell me," Lisa whispered, stroking Jordan's hair.

"Mommy," Jordan said choking back her tears, "Jesus came to me in my sleep."

"He did? What do you mean 'He came to me'?"

"I had this dream that I was walking in the temple in Jerusalem with Jesus, and He was holding my hand and smiling at me and telling me He loved me," Jordan blurted out with tears streaming down her face.

"The Roman soldiers then rushed toward us and took Him and

they were going to crucify Him! But Mommy, Jesus leaned down and put the nails in my hand and said, 'Jordan.' He put the hammer in my other hand and lifted me on His knee. He looked right into my eyes and said, 'Jordan, you have to do it.'"

Jordan sobbed uncontrollably trying to finish her story. "Mommy, I know what that means. Jesus was telling me that it was my sin that put Him on the tree," she whimpered.

Lisa held Jordan close and reassured her, "My precious little Jordan, I've never, ever had a dream like that, but I do believe that Jesus did want to touch a special place in your heart. It is about you, isn't it? It is about your sin."

"Yes, Mommy," Jordan said, slowly nodding her head. For the next several minutes Lisa comforted Jordan, reassuring her that Jesus loved her and gave her a tender heart to grieve over sin.

Moments like this one remind us that each of our children is blessed with different spiritual gifts, talents, temperaments, and interests. Our role as parents is to guide our children in their divine uniqueness and instill in them who God says they are.

how God sees us

Our children look like us *physically*, but what do they look like *spiritually*? Like Jesus! One way we remind our children that they look like Jesus is to meditate upon the "Who I Am in Christ" list compiled by seminary professor and counselor Neil Anderson. We want to give our children an identity based on God's truth, not the world's lies. To teach our children who God says they are, we wrote out Dr. Anderson's list on long sheets of butcher paper and stuck these sheets to the ceiling above their beds. Before they drift off to sleep, each child sees the words: "I am accepted. I am significant. I cannot be separated from the love of God."

We encourage your entire family to meditate on and even memorize these tremendous truths defining your God-given identity and personal significance.

who we are in Christ[3]

I Am Accepted

I am God's child. John 1:12

I am Christ's friend. John 15:15

I have been justified. Romans 5:1

I am united with the Lord, and am one spirit with Him.
1 Corinthians 6:17

I have been bought with a price. I belong to God.
1 Corinthians 6:19-20

I am a member of Christ's body. 1 Corinthians 12:27

I am a saint. Ephesians 1:1

I have been adopted as God's child. Ephesians 1:5

I have direct access to God through the Holy Spirit.
Ephesians 2:18

I have been redeemed and forgiven of all my sins.
Colossians 1:14

I am complete in Christ. Colossians 2:10

I Am Secure

I am free forever from condemnation. Romans 8:1-2

I am assured that all things work together for good.
Romans 8:28

I am free from any condemning charges against me.
Romans 8:31-34

I cannot be separated from the love of God.
Romans 8:35-39

I have been established, anointed, and sealed by God.
2 Corinthians 1:21-22

I am hidden with Christ in God. Colossians 3:3

I am confident that the good work God has begun in me
will be perfected. Philippians 1:6

I am a citizen of heaven. Philippians 3:20

I have not been given a spirit of fear, but of power, love,
and a sound mind. 2 Timothy 1:7

I can find grace and mercy in time of need. Hebrews 4:16

I am born of God; the evil one cannot touch me.
1 John 5:18

I Am Significant

I am the salt and light of the earth. Matthew 5:13-14

I am a branch of the true vine, a channel of His life.
John 15:1, 5

I have been chosen and appointed to bear fruit. John 15:16

I am a personal witness of Christ. Acts 1:8

I am God's temple. 1 Corinthians 3:16

I am a minister of reconciliation for God.
2 Corinthians 5:17-21

I am God's co-worker. 2 Corinthians 6:1

I am seated with Christ in the heavenly realm.
Ephesians 2:6

I am God's workmanship. Ephesians 2:10

I may approach God with freedom and confidence.
Ephesians 3:12

I can do all things through Christ who strengthens me.
Philippians 4:13

It's amazing to us how our children have taken these truths to heart. One of our favorite stories of this is when Khrysti came home one afternoon after inline skating in the neighborhood. She marched into the house with her hands on her hips, ponytails bouncing.

"Khrysti, how was skating?" we asked, noticing her determined look.

"It didn't go very well," she blurted out. "This little boy said I was stupid!"

"What did you say to him?" we asked.

"I told him, 'You may not speak to me like that! I am a child of Christ. I am redeemed. I'm a princess of the King!' So he said, 'Oh' and skated off."

We've taught our children not to fight with words but with God's truth. Truth sets us free—always. Psalm 119:42 shows us how to respond to others' harsh words based on our faith in God's Word: "Then I will answer the one who taunts me, for I trust in your word."

Our children love to review this spiritual identity list with each other. One night Randy heard Colten reading the "Who I Am in Christ" truths to Khrysti in her room. Three-year-old Khrysti sat on the bed sucking her thumb, taking it out occasionally to repeat a few phrases after her big brother.

Moving down the list, Khrysti suddenly chimed in, "I am a COW worker with Jesus!"

Smiling at our little girl's pronunciation, Randy briefly interrupted with, "No, honey, that's CO-worker."

Whether our kids correctly enunciate the words or not, night after night of reading who God says they are helps them stand up to the hurtful words of bullies and the temptation to follow after the world. Take a few minutes to write out this list for your children and watch God work mightily in their hearts and minds!

Randy's Purpose Statement

My purpose statement for this generation is to:
Cultivate my walk with God, the gifts of my
wife, Lisa, and the gifts of my children, Lauren,
Colten, Khrystian, Jordan, Logan, and Kameryn.

Cover my family, protecting them spiritually,
physically, and emotionally by building their
foundation on the Truth.

Call men to stand as high priests in their
homes being lovers, leaders, and loyal men.

Covenant with God and stand with Him to
count the cost and pass the Truth to the next
generation.

Complete the task and fulfill the purpose
that God created me for that He might be highly
exalted as the One and Only true God.

Randy Wilson,
Servant of God,
Husband of Lisa,
Father of Lauren, Colten, Khrystian, Jordan,
Logan, and Kameryn

Lisa's Purpose Statement

To know God deeply and make Him known through purposefully and passionately building our home on solid biblical truths. I will accomplish this through designing our days around the repetition and rehearsal of Scriptures and partnering with God to create moments that build faith and make Him the preeminence of all things.

To provide a loving environment for my children in a home that is a sanctuary. To build a home for the work of restoring, resting, rejoicing, reflecting, renewing, and reclaiming the Kingdom of God.

To use my God-given gifts to encourage women and mothers to love their calling, their homes, their husbands, and their families. To stand by Randy's side as I serve him as his Helper Completer in the fight for marriages and families.

By God's grace I will live out my purpose and impact my home, neighborhood, community, and world by proclaiming my love for my Lord and my God that will ripple throughout all of eternity.

TO GOD BE THE GLORY!

Lisa Wilson
August 29th, 1995

personal reflection

✿ What purpose do I want to fulfill as a parent?

✿ Do I truly understand who I am in Christ? How does this fuel my God-given purpose?

✿ Do I understand the transforming power and purpose of my spiritual identity?

✿ Do I walk in the authority of my identity and purpose and teach my children to do so?

✿ How can I help my kids understand their spiritual significance and purpose?

personal prayer

Father God, I pray that Your truth and the Scriptures that describe who we are when we enter Your kingdom will surround my children with holy boundaries. Help my children know, without a shadow of a doubt, who they are in You. May nothing and no one in the Enemy's camp discourage or confuse my kids about their spiritual identity. Guard my children to stand firm in their identity and the power and authority that You've already given them in the heavenlies. Remind them that they are children of the King—royalty because of You. Teach my children that they are in this generation to defend Your truth and to speak truth into the chaos of this world. May they walk regally and take Your mighty authority as a mantle upon their shoulders to defeat the enemy in the name of Jesus. Amen.

tools for creating your own celebration

    Long sheets of paper
    Marker or pen
    Thumb tacks or tape

16

Oaks of Righteousness

66 Solitary trees, if they grow
at all, grow strong. 99
—*Winston Churchill*[1]

66 Give me a place to stand,
and I will move the earth. 99
—*Archimedes*[2]

We tell each of our children, "You are not a willow, you are not a
birch, you are not an ash, you are not a maple, you are an oak tree.
You are an oak of righteousness because God says so. As a tall, sturdy
oak tree you are going to get hit by tough circumstances in life just
like mighty oak trees get hit by lightning. But you will stand strong."

"Why an oak tree?" they ask. So we tell them about one of our
mentor's favorite passages of Scripture, Isaiah 61:1-4:

> The Spirit of the Sovereign LORD is on me, because the
> LORD has anointed me to preach good news to the poor.
> He has sent me to bind up the brokenhearted, to proclaim
> freedom for the captives and release for the prisoners, to
> proclaim the year of the LORD's favor and the day of
> vengeance of our God, to comfort all who mourn, and

provide for those who grieve in Zion—to bestow on them
a crown of beauty instead of ashes, the oil of gladness
instead of mourning, and a garment of praise instead of a
spirit of despair. They will be called oaks of righteousness,
a planting of the LORD for the display of his splendor. They
will rebuild the ancient ruins and restore the places long
devastated; they will renew the ruined cities that have been
devastated for generations.

We particularly appreciate verse three where we are *"called oaks
of righteousness, a planting of the LORD for the display of his splendor."*
Why did God mention the oak tree instead of the giant cedars of
Lebanon? *Unger's Bible Dictionary* tells that in early times the oak was
a "consecrated tree," and people set up altars among oak groves
(Josh. 24:26). Others practiced idolatry under oaks (Isa. 1:29;
57:5) and carved idols out of oak (Isa. 44:14).[3] Still curious about
the oak tree, we discovered some amazing parallels between the
oak tree and the Christian life.

Known as the majestic monarchs of the forest, oak trees are a
symbol of majesty and power. *Christians stand strong in the
power of their almighty God.*

Oak trees may take more than one hundred years to reach maturity, but they live on for another nine hundred years. *Reach-
ing maturity in Christ is a process that God oversees in His time.*

Oaks were planted in public parks in the early days of America.
*God wants His children to branch out in the world and provide
shelter to those in need.*

Oak trees' sturdy hardwood was once used primarily for Navy
war vessels. *Christians are equipped with the armor of God to
win spiritual battles.*

Because oak trees tower (up to 150 feet high and four feet in
diameter) and often stand alone in open spaces, they are
struck by lightning more than any other tree. *Obedient followers of Christ may stand apart from the crowd in their beliefs
and face opposition, but they are never alone or forsaken.*

A medium-sized oak takes in up to 630 liters of water a day. *Every day believers are to drink from the Living Water to cleanse and refresh their souls.*

A single oak can support nearly three hundred different kinds of insects. *Every Christian is to be a life-giving source of hope and comfort to people from all walks of life.*

Oaks resprout readily but grow slowly. *God prunes Christians so they will steadily mature in faith year after year.*

Easily recognized by their fruit, the acorn, oaks do not usually produce acorns until they are about fifty years old, and then produce up to fifty thousand acorns a year. *Christians are identified by their fruit (Matt. 12:33) and are to "bear much fruit" (John 15:8).*

Oaks drop their leaves just before new leaves appear, and a mature oak sheds about a quarter million leaves every autumn. *Christians are to continually shed old habits and sins and grow in newness of life.*

Oak bark produces a substance called tannin, which is used as a preservative in leather. *Christians are to be salt and light (Matt. 5:13-14) to help preserve others from sin.*

No species of oak is immune to the deadly oak wilt fungus, which clogs a tree's water conduction vessels. Oak wilt easily spreads when the roots of infected neighboring trees graft onto the roots of healthy trees. *Christians are not immune to sin; that's why they must stand firm against attaching themselves to the ways of the world.*

To help our children understand their identity and purpose as "oaks of righteousness," Randy copied a drawing of an oak tree and wrote the Isaiah 61 verses around the tree. We framed this oak illustration and it hangs in our living room. This *Celebration of Faith* reminds our kids that they are not wilting weeds but majestic oak trees ready for God's service. Randy is also making each of our daughters a hope chest out of sturdy oak.

The example of the oak tree teaches our children to hold their heads high knowing they are "rooted and built up in him, strengthened in the faith as [they] were taught" (Col. 2:7). When we ponder the incredible nature of the oak tree, we tell our children, "Because of your faith, you're going to stand alone many times in life, but you're oaks of righteousness. Remember that. God is faithful. He is in you. Stand. Yes, you're going to take hits, but remember the Lord your God."

personal reflection

❀ Why does God refer to us as oak trees?
✿ What obstacles to faith are my children facing right now?
❀ How can we as a family rejoice in who we are, as a "display of His splendor"?

personal prayer

Father, may my children be the mighty monarchs of this generation. May they be the oaks that stand tall, not afraid to be hit by the lightning of the Enemy. May they bear much fruit and be signs of Your love, majesty, and righteousness. Help my young ones never waver in the foundations of Your truth. May they be preservatives in this culture and warfare vessels that conquer by the power of God invested in them. Lord, I commit my children as oaks of righteousness to You in the name of Jesus. Amen.

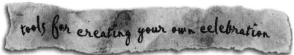

tools for creating your own celebration

Drawing or photo of oak tree
Writing of Isaiah 61:1-4 around the picture
Picture frame

17

Celebrate the Home

> **"**There is only one institution in the whole of society that undergirds, nourishes, promotes, and secures those very relationships we value most. That institution is the home. . . . As the home goes, so goes the woman.**"**
> —*Mary Farrar*[1]

One chilly, fall evening, a little boy selling candy bars knocked on our door. Randy chatted with Samuel and politely declined his sales offer. A few minutes later Samuel returned scared and distressed—a neighbor's dog nipped at him and several people had rudely turned him away. We warmed Samuel with hot chocolate as he waited on the curb for a van to pick him up.

After several more minutes, the van didn't show, so we invited the boy into our home. We quickly fixed shivering and hungry Samuel a snack and sat him by our toasty fireplace. He began to tell us about his gang- and drug-infested neighborhood in Denver. Our children sat wide-eyed, wondering why such a little boy would sell candy bars alone on such a dreary night. Randy asked the boy if he knew the meaning of the name Samuel and then told him about Samuel in the Bible.

As we continued to wait for the van, our family huddled around Samuel, and Randy prayed for God's protection and favor over him. When the van finally arrived, we all walked Samuel to the street, gave him our phone number, and hugged him good-bye.

That evening was not about keeping ourselves entertained by the fire, but about opening our home so our whole family could encourage a chilled and frightened little boy. We don't know if we'll ever entertain angels unaware, but we also don't know the needs of everyone coming to our door. What do people feel when they enter your home?

Several years ago Lisa did a study on what people in the Bible experienced when they entered women's homes:

Rahab, the harlot—a home of obedience and faith   (Josh. 2:1; 6:17, 22).
The widow with a jar of oil—a home of the ordinary, small things turned extraordinary (2 Kings 4:1-7).
The Shunamite—a home of rest (2 Kings 4:8-10).
Hannah—a home of worship and trust (1 Sam. 1).
Mary—a home of submission and reverence (Luke 1:26-30).
Elizabeth—a home of faith, rest, and waiting on God (Luke 1:39-41).
Mary and Martha—a home of welcome, worship, and fragrance (Luke 10:38-42).

Lydia—a home of an open, responsive heart (Acts 16:14-15).

But Lisa also found a contrasting view of the home in 2 Timothy 3:6-7: "For among them are those who enter into households and captivate weak women weighed down with sins, led on by various impulses, always learning and never able to come to the knowledge of the truth" (NASB). Lisa thought, *Would God enter my home and find a weak woman or a strong woman of faith? What would God sense when He enters our home?*

When others step into your home, do they find it captivated by weakness and "weighed down with sins"? Many homes today reflect this same chaos that Paul describes in 2 Timothy. Professor of Social Thought Allan Bloom says that sadly in many families, "the parent can no longer control the atmosphere of the home and has even lost the will to do so."[2]

A 1999 *USA Today* article about a Kaiser Family Foundation study of more than three thousand kids, ages two to eighteen, reports that: "The average kid in the USA spends five hours and twenty-nine minutes, seven days a week, watching TV, listening to music or working on a computer at home. And most of that is done in isolation—in bedrooms that are fully media-equipped—with no parental supervision."[3]

Michael and Diane Medved, in their book, *Saving Childhood,* note that the time Americans invest in watching television per week is "more time by age five than a child will spend talking to his father in a *lifetime.*"[4]

That's a sobering statistic! In many ways, media and high tech games have become idols in our homes. What is the atmosphere in your home? Are the kids typically glued to the television or computer? Is there anything you are allowing to enter your home that is captivating the hearts and minds of your children?

We cannot be fully present with our children or with guests who enter our home if we are distracted by gadgets and activities that limit authentic interaction with each other. Proverbs 7:11 describes a harried woman whose "feet do not remain at home." She sounds much like many mothers today who zip around from the mall to lunch to ball games to Bible studies, while their homes and families crumble from neglect. We have exchanged the mini civilization of the home for the civilization of the minivan!

Kansas mom Missy Trout spends three-and-one-half hours each day connected to other moms in cyberspace. "I live a good six-hour drive away from my family and friends," says Trout. "The ladies that I've met through ivillage.com have not only filled the gap, they are a source of escape, advice, inspiration, love, acceptance, and plain old adult conversation."[5]

While Missy is chatting on-line, what conversations and belly-laughter moments is she missing with her kids in the next room . . . her husband in the garage . . . and her neighbor next door?

beholding your children

Christ was a master at *beholding* people. Mark 10 says that Jesus beheld the rich young ruler and loved him. To behold means you "gaze upon" or carefully observe someone. God wants us to behold, or affix our attention upon our children and nurture them in a home filled with love, peace, and security. We cannot fully love our children until we *behold* our children.

The foundation of the home is the foundation of our culture, and what we do at home sets the tone for future generations. We behold our children when we focus on *kairos* moments with them. You are to be a life-giver to your children and in your home. Does your home invite an atmosphere to create and celebrate *kairos* moments with your children? To love our children, we must behold them—we must be fully present.

One of the *Celebrations of Faith* we want to pass on to our children is to rejoice in our home and secure it as a shelter of blessing for all who come inside. When you name something, you give it a purpose, so several years ago we named our home.

We had a brass plaque engraved with *The House of Blessings* and nailed it to our front door. Then we invited a few close friends over for a dedication ceremony where we committed our house to the Lord. Later, as a family, we walked around our property, from corner to corner, and dedicated it. We then anointed each room with oil as a sign of God's blessing. As a family we purposed in our hearts to live up to the name of our home—The House of Blessings.

foundation stones

Proverbs talks about two women—the woman of folly and the woman of wisdom. Proverbs 9:13-18 warns against going near the home of the woman of folly because she is "loud; she is undisciplined and without knowledge. . . . Her guests are in the depths of the grave." Those who enter her home are led astray and their spirits die.

In contrast, the woman of wisdom says, "Blessed is the man who listens to me, watching daily at my doors, waiting at my doorway. For whoever finds me finds life and receives favor from the LORD" (Prov. 8:34-35). The wise woman's home blesses others with God's favor.

To symbolize our desire to create a home of wisdom, truth, and God's favor, we bought two large garden stones inscribed with the words WISDOM and TRUTH. We placed the *Wisdom Stone* at our doorway because we want our children to know wisdom guards our doorway, not folly. As our family watched, Randy placed the *Truth Stone* on the hearth of our fireplace because in Latin "hearth" means focal point of the home. Day in and day out this visible symbol reminds our children that our home is founded on God's Truth.

If you think about your home growing up, certain objects were significant to you and you can still remember them. What symbols do you have in your home that your children will always remember? What do you want your home to be founded upon?

Exodus 10: 22-23 tells us that as part of the plagues, total darkness covered Egypt for three days, *yet light shone in all the Hebrew people's homes.* When God looked down through the thick darkness, He saw light in the homes of His people. What does God see when He looks down on your home? Do light and life shine from your home?

About a year ago, God showed us what even strangers see in our home. One afternoon Lisa sat on our front porch writing in her journal to God about how small and crowded our house is for eight people. Discouraged and lamenting, Lisa looked up to see a young woman stop on our sidewalk.

"Hi. Is this your house?" the woman cheerfully asked.

"Well, yes," Lisa replied, a bit surprised by the woman's question.

"I just want you to know that your house just glows. I'm new in the neighborhood, and every time I walk by here I notice how much light and warmth seem to radiate from your home."

Lisa and Alice began to chat and discovered that they both were Christians. "I just knew there was a presence of God when I came around your corner," Alice explained. "I'm not kidding. Your house just glows!"

Like Lisa, you may sometimes struggle with the size or style of your home, or you may question how God can use your home for His glory. But God's presence is always evident in the homes of those who follow Him. As God's people, we are "people of the light" (Luke 16:8), and we have His light in our homes whether we see it or not. Do your children know this? Celebrate your home and tell them!

Why not think of a special name for your "enlightened" home and dedicate your house for the Lord to build a solid legacy for the next generations. Together with your children, choose a symbol, like our *Wisdom* and *Truth Stones*, as a sign of the foundation of your home. Your home is worth celebrating!

❀ Do I give my best to my home and family or my best to the world?

❀ What do my children see in our home?

❀ What do others see when they enter our home?

❀ How can we make our home a place where God and others want to dwell?

❀ What name can we give to our home?

❀ How can we begin to celebrate our home?

In the name of Jesus, I pray a hedge of protection around our home. I ask that our family and home would be built through skillful and godly wisdom and understanding. May our home stand as a house of the righteous founded upon Jesus Christ. I pray that we would love each other and dwell securely in peace. May Your power and glory be evident, and may Your presence fill every room. We pray that we would love each other and dwell together in peace. When guests enter our home, may they leave with encouraged hearts and a deeper sense of Your holiness. Use our home to build a beautiful legacy of Your grace for generations to come. Amen.

tools for creating your own celebration

Plaque engraved with the name of your home
Large garden stones inscribed with foundational words
(wisdom, truth, peace, joy, for example)
Indelible marker or paint

18

Character Trophy

> "No person can consistently behave in a way that's inconsistent with the way he perceives himself."
> —*Neil T. Anderson*[1]

A tear edged its way down the towering man's face. Another tear followed before the broad-shouldered man rubbed a callused hand across his weathered cheeks. "He's talking about *my* boy," he mumbled. "That's *my* Daniel."

"Daniel . . . Daniel . . . Daniel!" chanted the entire sixth grade classroom that afternoon in March. "He's The Wall. . . . He's The Wall!" the rambunctious gang roared, squirming and jumping from their seats.

At the front of the room a stocky brown-haired boy clutched a trophy, beaming like the proud winner of the Tour de France. That's Daniel, the kid none of his classmates seemed to like—that is, until that winter afternoon.

As the goalie on Colten's hockey team, Daniel wore a tough exterior almost as thick as his game-day padding. His classmates feared him as critical, sarcastic, and disrespectful of authority. But none of them knew Daniel as our family came to know him.

As the hockey team's coach, Randy began to soften Daniel's

defiant heart with unconditional love and genuine encouragement. After the team won the league championship game, thanks in large part to Daniel's dogged defense at the net, Randy wanted to honor this misunderstood eleven year old.

Randy bought a gold trophy with a goalie on top and inscribed with Daniel's name and the nickname the team gave their power-house goalie: The Wall. Colten and our three older girls decorated a huge banner with "Daniel Is a Champion! He's a Wall!" Randy asked Daniel's school for permission to present Daniel with this trophy and banner before his classmates. Even Daniel's father showed up to see another side to his troubled son.

Randy told the packed classroom about Daniel's noble and persevering character and how he shone as an athlete. Suddenly this unpopular boy became a real-life hero to his peers and a treasured son to his proud dad. Overcoming years of teasing and rejection, The Wall continued to stand. Daniel taught us all about honoring someone's true character.

Paying tribute to Daniel's persevering character gave us the idea to design a *Character Trophy* for each of our children. Our names and the character qualities we model are a significant part of God's plan for each of us. Our names help give us meaning and purpose. Isaiah 49:1 says, "Before I was born the LORD called me; from my birth he has made mention of my name."

God knew our names before we were born, and He blessed each of us with unique personalities and gifts. Do you know the meaning of your name? Do you know the meaning of your children's names? If you want to find out, libraries and bookstores carry dozens of name books. (Just ask any expectant parent!)

We first gave a *Character Trophy* to our oldest child, Lauren, when she was around ten years old. We had a Christian woman in the trophy business engrave a large golden cup mounted on a marble-like stand with *Lauren Brooke, Victorious One, One Who Perseveres.* On the back of the trophy we engraved the life verse we selected to match Lauren's name: "I can do everything through him who gives me strength" (Phil. 4:13).

We plan to award each one of our children with a *Character Trophy* uplifting his or her name and character. The timing of this depends on the age at which each child truly shows a particular character trait and consistently models this attribute in day-to-day life.

You may have a child like Daniel who endures despite pressures from the world. The small investment in a *Character Trophy* will boost this child's self esteem for a lifetime. Celebrate who your children really are!

personal reflection

❀ What do the names of each member of my family mean?

❀ What character qualities do each of my children demonstrate?

❀ How can we as a family honor each other's names and
   character traits?

personal prayer

Father, I pray that I would exalt the blessing and beauty of my children's names and who they are. My children are precious in Your sight, and You knew their names before they were born. In fact, Psalm 139 says You search them and You are familiar with all their ways. I pray that You would call out the beauty and the holiness of the character You are forming in my children's spirits. As a parent, I am depending on You for wisdom, understanding, and strength in how to guide my children in who You created them to be. You are the divine Maker of hearts and character. I celebrate the noble names and characters of Your precious gifts to me—my children. In Your name I pray. Amen.

tools for creating your own celebration

Source to find meaning of names

A Scripture to describe your child or the child's life verse

Engraved trophy or symbolic award

You can also purchase business cards printed with your
child's name, life verse, and your phone number and
address. Give the cards to friends.

19

Wisdom Teas

> **"Train the younger women to love their husbands and children, to be self-controlled and pure."**
> —*Titus 2:4-5*

Crumpled on my bedroom floor with tears cascading down my cheeks, I felt so inadequate as a mother. *How can I lead my daughter in her teen years? I don't have the same gifts as her, and I don't think like her,* I cried out to God in prayer. Lauren shows such strength in organization, piano, sewing, ballet, and serving others that I feared because I don't share her same gifts, I couldn't help her enhance her skills.

But that morning as I poured out my concerns to God, He nudged me with the idea of finding other women to help mentor my daughter. Together as older women we could collectively share our talents with our young daughters. We need each other as women, and I wanted other women to guide all four of my girls and help pull out areas of giftedness that were opposite of mine.

I love the story of the young maiden Mary right after the angel told her she had conceived the Son of God in her womb. For years she listened to the Holy Scriptures and rabbis in the temple. Her young heart and spirit were full of deep, rich truths of God. God had prepared her spirit for the wondrous news of delivering the Messiah to the world, yet what did God do? He sent Mary to visit Elizabeth, so this wise mentor could rub Mary's back, make her tea, and reassure her that life would turn out okay. Mary enjoyed three months of sitting at the feet of another woman!

Although Mary carried the all-sufficient God of the universe inside her, she still needed an older woman to sit with and talk to heart-to-heart. God in His wisdom knew nothing was more important at that time than to send this expectant teen to the comforting arms of another woman. God carefully crafts women with hearts to encourage and counsel other women.

In my early days of desperate and exhausted motherhood, I picked out a few women of faith whom I saw as strong role models as wives and mothers. I would take a notepad to their homes and ask questions about parenting and jot down their wise words. I'd observe these women in church and see how they worshiped and spoke to their husbands and loved their children. Because I've often looked to other women in my life for advice and inspiration, I want to be sure my daughters learn how to benefit from godly mentors too.

I'm so amazed at the wise and wonderful mentors God has placed in my life:

Deb—my friend of thirty-five years who models godliness in all seasons of life.

Bev—her gift of hospitality gives life to so many others.

Annie—I always left her house singing.

Bev S.—a prayer warrior who models obedience.

Cynthia—her beauty inside and out refreshes my heart.

Judy—her graceful mothering skills and radiant smile feed my weary heart.

Phyllis—her love for truth makes me hunger for more.

Kay—her grace and humility honor God.

I've also benefited from studying the lives of great women of faith including Susanna Wesley, Sarah Edwards, Mary Washington, Madame Guyon, Hannah Whitall Smith, Catherine Marshall, Corrie Ten Boom, and Elisabeth Elliot.

I wanted to encourage women with skills of hand and skills of heart to come into my daughters' lives. So I purposely looked for godly, older women who were willing to share their wisdom and expertise with young girls. (Randy did the same with male mentors, which he shares in chapters twenty-three and twenty-four.) I wrote a letter to other mothers and daughters explaining my idea, and from that a mentoring group started in our home.

Once a month I began hosting *Wisdom Teas*, where older women taught my daughters and their friends specific life skills. The informal teas created opportunities for the girls to ask these seasoned women about walking with God through everyday joys and challenges.

Over the years our small group has grown to about seventy girls who now meet in our church weekly for mentoring. The girls have learned about floral design, photography, journaling, interior decorating, calligraphy, beauty tips, nutrition, and so much more. My goal is to stir up skills of heart and skills of hand in the lives of our daughters. Here are some of the questions we've explored during our sessions:

How did you meet Jesus?

Who is your favorite woman Bible character and why?

Who is your favorite lady in history?

What is your counsel on preparing for teen years and looking toward building a godly home?

What is the most important quality you find in a friend?

What one woman has influenced your life the most and why?

What is your favorite quote?

What is your favorite Scripture?

Who is your favorite worship music and/or artist?

Who is your favorite author and what is your favorite book in these areas:

History _____

Devotional_____

Fiction _____

Biography/Autobiography_____

Home management _____

Child rearing _____

Marriage _____

Other _____

What skill is being taught?
What have I learned from this skill?

In addition to the hands-on skill lessons, the girls meet for Bible study and a video night during which we view movie clips and discern how the women line up with Scripture. We discuss the movie's main female character and the feminine aspect she portrays. We think of other female characters who remind us of this woman. We also discuss how we are similar and different from this character and what we can learn from her.

Our weekly group ended our first year together with an extravagant *Father-Daughter Ball* (see chapter twenty-two). I still host smaller *Wisdom Teas* from time to time in our home, and I hope you'll give one a try. Like young Mary experienced centuries ago, there's nothing quite like resting at the feet of someone who's already smoothed a path for you to follow. There's nothing like the heart of a woman!

✿ Who are the godly women mentors in my life?
✿ What would I like my daughter to learn from these women?
✿ How can I encourage other women to pass on specific skills to my daughter?
✿ What models from history do I want to introduce to my daughter?

Father, may my daughter be transformed through the presence of older role models and mentors in her life. Thank You for the deep treasures stored up in the hearts of older women. May my daughter be forever changed by the richness and depth of beauty of these women who for years have pondered and treasured worthy and powerful things. Help my daughter humbly receive from the teaching and the skills of hearts and hands from these wise mentors. May my girl grow into a beautiful, godly princess for Your kingdom through everything she learns from these women of worth. Stir more women to mentor and model Your godliness and holiness to each other and to all our daughters. In Jesus' name, amen.

A Scriptural Blessing for Daughters

I bless you, My beautiful daughter. I want you to know you are beautiful; I made you. I mentioned your name at your birth. You were in My thoughts before the beginning of time. I formed you in your mother's womb. I chose the color of your hair, your eyes, your smile, your voice, your body shape, the way you think, the way you walk. I gave you personality, your skills, your gifts, your passions, your ability to love and be loved.

I am your Father. I love you with an everlasting love. I love you—you are mine! I am jealous for you and your heart. Guard your heart! My eyes never leave you. I carry you in My heart. I cover you under the shadow of My wings, so you can be covered, feel safe and secure. I am your tower of strength; run to Me; let Me be your refuge. I am your comforter. Run to My heart. I am the lover of your soul. Rest in My love. Let Me love you. I smile when I watch you laugh. I know every tear you've ever cried. I've engraved you in the palm of My hand. I adore you, My daughter.

I send angels to watch over you and minister to you. You are My princess. I crown you with loving kindness and life. I always have time for you. I will never, ever, no never leave you or let you down—NEVER!

When you feel alone, sad, angry, depressed, or empty inside, I'm right beside you, loving you, and gently holding you. You are My beloved treasure, My creation, My delight, and the fragrance of My heart. Come to Me. Let Me love you. I love you My beautiful child.

Your Heavenly Father,
God

tools for creating your own celebration

Group of spiritually mature women mentors
Girls who are open to learning fun and practical skills
Inspiring videos of women who model biblical principles
Place to meet regularly
Biographies, autobiographies of female role models in history

20

Legacy Tea

"The woman at whose domestic hearth, and by whose judicious maternal love, a family of industrious, godly, and public-spirited sons, or of modest, kindhearted, prudent, and pious daughters, is trained for future life, is an ornament of her country, a benefactress to her species, and a blessing to posterity."
—John Angell James[1]

"I love God. God loves you. So by the transitive property of geometry, I love you!" is scrawled inside the cover of my tattered Bible from junior high. When I wrote this lighthearted saying in my much-cherished Bible back in the '70s, I no idea I would someday view my blue Bible as a keepsake to pass on to my children. But now this worn treasure rests in my oldest daughter's hope chest, and I remember the special day I gave it to her at our first *Legacy Tea*.

At the end of our first year mentoring moms and daughters, I wanted to recognize the twelve-to-fourteen year olds with a *Legacy Tea*, to give the girls a vision of their beauty in this generation and to give them a sense of the power of the women's lives who walked with God before them. One's legacy always begins with a purpose and reveals a purpose, and I wanted to create a moment in the girls' lives for an eternal vision.

The tea was a memorable formal affair replete with gorgeous dresses, fine china, glowing candles, savory teas, and gourmet desserts. My lovely friend Kay opened her home to us and shared her journey of soul and her journey of marriage and motherhood. Each mother and daughter brought their own teacups or tea pot and told stories behind each piece. Each family also brought a delectable dessert to share.

In the invitations I asked each mother to surprise her daughter with a gift-wrapped family heirloom. Around the room tears flowed as these moms told heart-warming stories behind their heirloom gifts.

Each girl was asked to write a letter to her future husband and children about her intent to remain pure and walk with God through her teen years. If they wanted, the girls could read aloud these letters at the tea.

During the legacy celebration, the girls signed these letters and their mothers signed them as witnesses. The letters were sealed to be opened when the girls later step into marriage. Below are the letters Lauren wrote to her future husband and children.

May 13, 1997

My dearest husband,

I am preparing myself now for being a godly wife by reading the Bible, praying often, and learning home living skills (hospitality, organization, beauty, etc.) The qualities I pray you will have are:

Purity

A love for God

A servant spirit

A love for children

And one who perseveres.

My dad has a great love for Mom and his children. He works very, very hard. He gets up at 3:45 A.M. just to pray and spend time with God before work. He gives up anything he wants to do just to spend all the time he can with his family. He blesses us every Sunday and always tells us he loves us! I pray that you will be like him too!

I have given my heart to God and to my dad so that I can save it for you, and I will keep my heart pure. The Scripture I want to live by is Psalm 101:2-3: "I will be careful to lead a blameless life . . . I will walk in my house with a blameless heart. I will set before my eyes no vile thing."

I promise to be your crown and be your glory for as long as I live. I promise to be the best wife I can be to you.

Love, your wife,
Lauren

May 13, 1997

Dear Children,

As I sit to write this, I am more eager to meet you! I am now preparing myself for motherhood as I take care of my little brother and sister. I *love watching them grow up, and they are teaching me a lot about mothering.*

I pray I'll be the best mom I can be with God's help. I promise to love you and care for you always.

Children, I ask God to help me teach you obedience, prayer, Scripture, and to love the Lord your God with all your heart, soul, and mind, and to come to know Him at an early age.

I pray we can be close to each other for as long as we live. I pray that God will touch your little lives at an early age. I pray that every step you take as you grow up will be pleasing to God.

As it says in Proverbs: "Train up a child in the way he should go, and when he is old he will not depart from it." That is what I am going to do with you!

God has already planned you and has a special purpose for you, and I can't wait to see what that is!

Love,
Lauren

Either by convenience or conviction, or by default or by decision, we are creating a legacy for our daughters. Let's join together in creating a legacy for our daughters that will honor our Creator from now until we meet Him face to face.

personal reflection

❀ What vision do I have for my daughter entering her teen
   years?
❀ What kind of legacy am I creating?
❀ How am I facilitating that vision?
❀ What other mothers and daughters can spur us on in faith?
❀ What books, videos, or conferences do I plan for my
   daughter and me to read, watch, and attend?
❀ How can I celebrate creating a legacy with my daughter?

personal prayer

Father, thank You for the power of a legacy. May my daughter never forget what has been passed down to her. May she be a keeper of the beauty of memories. Help my daughter treasure the legacy that I am imparting to her. May she choose to follow You all the days of her life. Protect me from passing down worthless idols to my daughter. Allow me to teach her the true knowledge of You who can redeem lives for generations to come by Your power and love. Father, my girl is precious, and I commit her to You in the holy name of Jesus. Amen.

tools for creating your own celebration

   Desserts and teas
   Tea serving sets
   Heirloom gifts
   Letters written to future spouses and children

21

Chayil Celebration

" A wife of noble character who can find? She is worth far more than rubies. **"**
—*Proverbs 31:10*

The whirring saw and pounding hammer reverberated from the garage those chilly winter days, but the sounds I remember most are the laughter and singing of my husband and oldest daughter. Occasionally I'd interrupt Randy and Lauren's woodworking endeavor with hot cocoa and cookies, then slip back inside the house knowing that someday we'd celebrate the grand unveiling of their project—Lauren's oak hope chest.

This father-daughter adventure was part of honoring Lauren's passage into her teen years. In Hebrew, *chayil* means "virtuous woman." *Chayil* signifies a covenant of purity and purpose. We designed a *Chayil Celebration* to mark our daughters' journey into womanhood at age thirteen. We initiated this celebration with Lauren.

I invited about thirty women and a few of Lauren's close friends to witness the event in our home and bring a symbolic gift to encourage Lauren to grow into a strong woman of faith. The adults were godly women in the community who had personally influenced Lauren. The year leading up to this significant event, Lauren learned a skill that would take her into adulthood—she worked on a quilt that we displayed at the celebration.

During the ceremony, Lauren received spoken blessings and gifts such as pearl earrings to remind Lauren she is a pearl of great price. A gift of a brick covered in velvet symbolized that a virtuous woman is strong but gentle. I gave Lauren the well-worn Bible from my teen years, and she received letters of blessing from family that could not attend. Lauren also read this purpose statement that she wrote for her teen years:

Daughter's Purpose and Purity Covenant

Lord,

I purpose to love You with all my heart, soul, and mind. And I would like You to help me grow deeper in the Bible and to grow closer to You in my teen years.

I purpose to do my best in obeying my parents. Please help me grow even closer to them during my teen years.

I purpose to do my best with my brothers and sisters. Please help me be even more loving and patient toward them.

I purpose to stay pure until marriage.

I purpose to keep my thoughts pure with Your help.

I purpose to keep my eyes and ears pure with Your help.

I purpose to choose wise friends with Your help and Mom and Dad's help.

> *I purpose to stay focused on You and on Your path You laid out for me.*
>
> *I purpose to spend time with godly women who will encourage and teach me in godly womanhood.*
>
> *I purpose to seek to learn skills and set my heart on preparing for a godly home as a wife and mother.*
>
> Signed_____ Date _____
>
> Witnesses _____ Date _____

Together Randy and I selected various symbols to remind Lauren that we are committed to helping her transition into adulthood. Proverbs 4:23 says, "Above all else, guard your heart, for it is the wellspring of life." As each of our daughters reach their teen years, we want to help them guard their hearts from unhealthy choices, especially in the area of relationships. The following symbols represent Lauren's covenant of purity and purpose.

hope chest

Lauren and Randy built an oak hope chest together, and Randy used a wood burner to engrave the inside lid with Deuteronomy 7:9: "He is the faithful God, keeping his covenant of love to a thousand generations of those who love him."

purity ring

During the ceremony, Randy presented Lauren with her *grandmother's ring* as a reminder of God's design of purity through all generations. We also displayed photos of five generations of godly women relatives who walked in integrity and purity before Lauren.

purity necklace

We gave Lauren a sterling silver necklace with special charms as symbols of purity.

A lock and key represent physical purity. Randy took the key to guard her purity now and will present the key to her husband on her wedding day.

A silver heart symbolizes guarding her heart to be pure emotionally and not quick to give her heart away before the right man.

A mustard seed encourages Lauren to keep pure in her faith.

A silver envelope represents a sealed covenant she wrote to her future husband and children. She will open these letters on her wedding day and the day her first child is born.

A silver baby shoe reminds Lauren of her promise to be pure for the next generation. She'll give this charm to her first baby.

crown of wisdom

To represent our desire for Lauren to walk in the wisdom of Proverbs, I made her a garland of silk flowers and pearls with long ribbons hanging down the back. Six gems that look like rubies line the inside of the crown to remind Lauren that her worth is far above rubies (Prov. 31:10). These "rubies" represent three skills of Lauren's heart—fearing the Lord, faithful in small things, serving others—and three skills of her hand—art, organization, music.

foot washing bowl

We honored Lauren's spiritual gift of serving by giving her a white ceramic foot washing bowl and ceramic pitcher with a towel embroidered with her name. Lauren can carry these symbols of servanthood into her home someday.

alabaster box

In the Hebrew tradition, the fathers of young virgins saved up about a year's salary to purchase an alabaster box and fill it with fragrant oil. When a maiden's future husband was accepted into the family, she broke her alabaster box at his feet. We found an ornate pressed coral box and placed a tiny vial of oil in it along with a letter that Randy wrote to Lauren's future husband. Randy's letter bestows honor and blessing upon our future son-in-law and tells him of our years of prayers for him. Randy will anoint this young man with the oil when he asks for Lauren's hand in marriage and Randy gives his permission.

Below is Randy's letter that Lauren keeps in her "alabaster" box.

> *Dear Son-in-law,*
>
> *By the time you sit down and read this the wedding day will have passed. All the plans to put you on this new road will be a memory now, and there is nothing but a great future ahead of you and Lauren.*
>
> *I know we have had long talks about Lauren, but let me write them down so you can refer to them on some days you might forget. It seems like yesterday she was a giggling little girl exploring her new world, protecting her doll, and trying on another one of Mom's dresses.*
>
> *Lauren has always shown us a deep love for her God, an incredible sense of right and wrong, great responsibility, and a servant's heart. She has an amazing eye for beauty and a need to surround*

herself with beauty. Lauren's heart is full to overflowing with love and care for others and she will
smother you with that love and care. She is very
unselfish almost to a fault. Be aware of this and
protect her from others who will take advantage
of her unselfishness. She waits for your leadership
and will respond to you accordingly.

Lauren has great inner strength and physical
stamina, but she will need your God-given
strength to function. In my conversations with
her, she wants to please you like no other. Know
this and stay alert. Listen to her. Look deep into
her eyes and listen. Even though nothing is being
said, she will speak to you with her eyes.

Like no other now, Lauren is yours. Life is
about you and Lauren and no one else. It is you
and she who will make decisions about your lives.
No one else knows what you do. Yes, I am still
here and available, as is Lisa, your mom and
dad, but you are responsible for all decisions.
Surround yourselves with mentors, strong people
who will listen and give you feedback. People that
will support your purpose and mission in life.

Most importantly, Lauren needs your spiritual
leadership. She needs you to take her to the
throne of God, to pray with her, to lead her in
understanding and growing in Christ. The life
now before you two is awesome, huge, and full of

opportunity. It is also bigger than yourselves. Don't forget, God is already doing great things around you, and He wants to involve you. He will grow you up through pain, through stretching that will be uncomfortable at times. Also remember He loves you more than anyone could and is working in you for a purpose, a purpose you were created for.

Forgiveness is key to the day-to-day enjoyment of each other's company. You will find if there is unforgiveness from you or from Lauren, the joy of life will be gone. Just like broken fellowship between you and God stops your fellowship, so unforgiveness stops fellowship between you and Lauren. Your life will flourish or dissolve, overflow with love and joy or discouragement and despair depending on your relationship with God and Lauren.

I commit to pray for you and will always be available to you. I commit to you that I will not interfere with your leadership. I entrust you in the hands of our almighty God and relinquish one of my most treasured possessions, Lauren. May God fill you with the fullness of His mighty love, mercy, and grace. May He grant you His wisdom, understanding, and strength to stand courageously against the wiles of the evil one. May you be as strong as a lion and as harmless as

*a dove and know His purpose for you, Lauren, and
your children to come. The Lord bless you and
keep you, the Lord make His face shine upon you
and turn His face toward you, and give you peace.*

blessing and anointing with oil

During the *Chayil Celebration*, Lauren knelt before Randy and he anointed her with oil and blessed her in her journey through her teen years. She sang a song she dedicated to us as a pledge of her purity and read a purity vow she made to God. We closed with everyone holding hands and praying together and singing "Great Is Thy Faithfulness."

In the years to come, we will honor our younger daughters with their own "virtuous woman ceremony" tailored to their individual personalities and strengths. Our daughters' purity is not just about their purity in the present—the choices they make now will affect the hearts of their children for generations.

We encourage you to honor the gift of purity and purpose as your little girls grow into noble women of faith. Together may we raise virtuous young girls to become virtuous young women—who will stand like no generation that has ever lived before—to defend the righteous beauty of living pure lives before God and others.

personal reflection

❀ What does the Bible say about living in purity?

✿ How can I begin now to teach my little girl about God's design for purity?

How can we celebrate my daughter's passage into womanhood?

What are her unique passions, bents, and gifts we wish to
celebrate?

personal prayer

Lord, I bring my daughter and her commitment to purity
to Your throne. I pray for the purpose of her heart to stay
pure not only in body, but also in mind, heart, attitudes,
and deeds. May she follow Your higher calling of purity and
not give in to cultural pressures to conform. I ask that the
Enemy would have no place in her mind and heart. May
you lead a godly husband into her life to love her like
Christ does. Together may this couple celebrate the power,
majesty, and beauty of purity in their marriage and teach
their children of Your perfect ways. Thank You for the privilege of celebrating purity, and I commit this protection of
the purity of my daughter into the hands of my holy God.
In Your precious name I pray. Amen.

tools for creating your own celebration

Purity symbols (ring, charms, for example) that are
unique to your daughter
Letter of purity pledge by daughter
Letter to future son-in-law by father

22

Father-Daughter Purity Ball

> **"**All glorious is the princess within.**"**
> —Psalm 45:13

> **"**You will be a crown of splendor
> in the Lord's hand, a royal diadem
> in the hand of your God.**"**
> —Isaiah 62:3

"The moment I put my hand in my father's, I felt like a princess. In those six precious hours, I believe I grew in relationship with my father more than I ever have. I knew it was my night, and I treasured every minute of it," said eleven-year-old Anna Tullis of our *Father-Daughter Purity Ball*.

"Dancing with my dad was the most wonderful part of the evening. As we waltzed around the ballroom, he would speak blessings into my life," exclaimed Anna's fourteen-year-old sister, Sarah. "I realized what a privilege it was to be able to spend a night with my dad as he imparted glory and purity into my life."

And how did these girls' father feel about this stellar evening with his daughters in the Grand Ballroom of the world famous Broadmoor Hotel?

"How can you measure the value of your eleven year old looking up into your eyes (as you clumsily learn the fox-trot together) with innocent, uncontainable joy, saying, 'Daddy, I'm so excited!'" wrote Wesley Tullis in a letter describing his grateful participation. "I have been involved with the Father-Daughter Ball for two years with my daughters, Sarah and Anna. It is impossible to convey what I have seen in their sweet spirits, their delicate, forming souls, as their daddy takes them out for their first, big dance. Their whole being absorbs my loving attention, resulting in a radiant sense of self-worth and identity. Think of it from their perspective:

> My daddy thinks I'm beautiful in my own unique way.
> My daddy is treating me with respect and honor.
> My daddy has taken time to be silly, and even made a fool of
>   himself, learning how to dance.
> My daddy *really* loves me!"

The Tullis family is one of dozens of families who joined us for our second *Father-Daughter Purity Ball* on April 7, 2000, in Colorado Springs, Colorado. What a spectacular night of tribute to the covenant of purity! Families from fourteen churches in Colorado Springs, three other Colorado cities, and two additional states attended this evening of extravagant celebration.

We know God was pleased with our magnificent ceremony because it is God Himself who bestows lavish fanfare on the gift of purity. We see this in Bible times as young Hebrew virgins followed an extravagant premarriage custom. In the last chapter, we discussed how the maidens' fathers saved a year's salary to buy expensive alabaster boxes and perfumed oil to honor their future sons-in-law. In God's eyes, protecting one's purity is a holy covenant, worthy of glorious celebration! The protection of purity should be extravagant!

A *Father-Daughter Purity Ball* is a memorable ceremony for daughters to pledge commitments to purity and their fathers to pledge commitments to protect their girls. Because we cherish our daughters as regal princesses—for 1 Peter 3:4 (NASB) says they are "precious in the sight of God"—we want to treat them as royalty. To commemorate our daughters' vows of purity, we and several other parents chose to honor our girls not with burgers and a back-yard barbecue, but with a banquet in a five-star hotel ballroom.

For six months leading up to the ball, our daughters saved their money for elegant ball gowns and joyfully daydreamed about the spring celebration. Many girls, including our Khrystian and Jordan, practiced ballet for the ball. We also arranged ballroom dance lessons for the fathers and daughters to prepare them for their special night.

A *Father-Daughter Purity Ball* is an incredible dedication of beauty and grace. We decorate every table with a different calligraphy banner describing the feminine spirit: gentleness, purity, graciousness, kindness, beautiful, precious, a treasure, helper/completer, and life-giver.

The ball's program includes inspiring worship ballet and musical tributes performed by several daughters. Our dear friend and ballet instructor Patty choreographed a beautiful sequence of songs, setting the tone for the evening. The songs displayed the divine order—celebrate God, celebrate fathers, celebrate daughters, celebrate life. The beauty was simply indescribable! All of heaven must have watched in hushed tones.

As a couple, we present messages on the beauty of daughters and a father's call to covenant. We call the girls to stand as centerpieces in our culture and to seriously regard their purity and holiness. We admonish the fathers to war for their daughters—for their purity, their souls, their physical well-being, and for their hearts. Together the daughters and fathers sign covenants of purity and protection. (We've included a sample of this covenant at the end of the chapter.)

One of the most memorable highlights of the ball is when the fathers stand in the middle of the ballroom and form a circle around their daughters standing all aglow in their lovely ball gowns. The fathers place their hands on their daughters, and together we pray for purity of mind, body, and soul for generations to come. What a breathtaking moment before the Lord and His rapturous angels. The covering of protection by the fathers is so pleasing to God, the Father.

Our dear friend Wesley Tullis describes this soul-stirring portion of the ball: "Such an impregnable wall of fathers is what is necessary to see a movement grow that changes the course of our nation's history. I stand with Randy Wilson and the men of my church, city, and nation to see such a movement occur."

We cap off the evening with ballroom dancing until midnight. During dance breaks, many of the girls spontaneously grab a microphone and proudly thank and bless their fathers. Several fathers respond by coming to the microphone and humbly asking for forgiveness for their weaknesses and vowing with God's help to honor and protect their girls. No society page could adequately cover the depth of joy and love expressed at a *Father-Daughter Purity Ball*!

However you design a purity celebration for daughters and fathers, we encourage you to plan extravagantly. God is pleased when we join together to bestow beauty and honor on the covenants of purity and protection. Let the celebration begin!

Purity Covering and Covenant

I,_____'s father, choose before God to cover my daughter as her authority and protection in the area of purity. I will be pure in my own life as a man, husband, and father. I will be a man of integrity and accountability as I lead, guide, and pray over my daughter and my family as the high priest in my home. This covering will be used by God to influence generations to come.

Signed_____ Date_____

Daughter _____

personal reflection

- What does it mean to protect the purity of my daughter?
- How am I protecting my daughter's heart?
- How can I consistently plan one-on-one time with my daughter?
- Do I know what her greatest fears are?
- Does she know that I see her as a beautiful princess?
- Does she see herself as beautiful?
- Am I holding her as the man in her life?
- Are my hugs and touch protecting her heart as a young woman?
- Am I protecting her fragile heart from the boys?
- Am I asking my daughter if she feels protected?
- In what areas does she feel unprotected?
- Does my daughter know that, as her dad, I am to protect her and will someday transfer that protection to her husband?

personal prayer for fathers

Heavenly Father, I make a covenant with my eyes to keep them pure and to keep them from looking where I should not look. Give me discernment to see and understand the needs of my daughter. Help me regard her need for security and protection for her purity physically, emotionally, and spiritually. Give me strength to cover her in each of these areas. Grant me Your wisdom to know what questions to ask her. Help me to stay connected with her heart and to be the man in her life until You bring the man You created to become her husband. In Jesus' name, amen.

personal prayer for a father-daughter purity ball

Lord, in the name of Jesus we commit this evening to You. We thank You that we have the privilege of planning a ceremony that extravagantly protects purity. We thank You that in Your Scriptures the protection of purity was extravagant and beautiful, and we pray that these girls will never forget this evening with their fathers. Our daughters are princesses, and they are covered by the authority and headship of their fathers. We pray a wall of protection around our girls that they would not give in to a moment that would destroy their lives. Father, guard the feminine, vulnerable, dependent spirits that You created in them. May fathers stand tall and war for the souls of their daughters and remain faithful to protect these girls for generations to come. Amen.

tools for creating your own celebration

Ballroom or large meeting room
Appropriate decorations
Ballroom dance music
Reception food and drinks
Special entertainment (vocalists, ballerinas, for example)
Printed covenants and programs
Prayer!

23
Celebration of Manhood

"Boys become men by watching men, by standing close to men. Manhood is a ritual passed from generation to generation with precious few spoken instructions. Passing the torch of manhood is a fragile, tedious task. If the rite of passage is successfully completed, the boy-become-man is like an oak of hardwood character. His shade and influence will bless all those who are fortunate enough to lean on him and rest under his canopy.**"**
—*Preston Gillham*[1]

"I took off my uniform and started for the showers, and standing over at the far wall was my dad. He had been there for two-and-a-half hours and he had not come into my cubicle. We locked eyes. He stood up straight and said to me, 'Hey, great game!' I burst into tears. Compliments from my dad never had been easy coming, and I reached out and we hugged each other. *From that moment*, I knew my dad."[2]

Mark Harmon, former NFL quarterback, shares these words

about the first time he and his father truly connected as father and son. For many of us, this moment never comes. In our culture today, many boys grow physically into men, but emotionally and spiritually they remain juveniles. Our role as fathers is to help our sons transition into manhood fully prepared as God's choice warriors.

Because the defining line between childhood and manhood is often indistinguishable in our world, I want to show my sons a clear line they can cross to enter manhood. A few years ago, I mapped out a course with our oldest son, Colten.

I chose to mark his step into manhood at age twelve—the same age Jesus first questioned rabbis and discussed the Scriptures in His Father's house—with a celebration called *Brave Heart of a Warrior*. (We discussed a man's call to be a warrior in chapter three.) The purpose of this celebration is to mark in time, to raise a monument, that testifies that our sons have crossed a threshold that separates boyhood from manhood.

"Ritual rites of passage . . . is the one most rich in communal input," explains Michael Gurian in *The Wonder of Boys*. "In its ideal, a church ceremony, a rite of passage adventure, an event a group or family creates for itself, has four main components: a safe place, trusted elders, a prepared ritual accepted by the community, a ritual imbued with sacred energy and tradition."[3]

the ceremony

For a year leading up to this coming-of-age event, I asked Colten to study the life and character of one man in history who honored God. Colten chose George Washington, first president of the United States. Colten read books and articles on this man of faith and synthesized an overview of Washington's life into a oral presentation, "The Life and Times of George Washington." He delivered this fascinating oratory at his manhood ceremony.

I invited about thirty men and friends of Colten's to attend Colten's *Brave Heart of a Warrior* celebration. These men are my mentors, peers I am accountable to, and men I mentor myself. I asked each of these men to share insights and experiences with Colten during the ceremony and to walk alongside Colten as he continues to grow into maturity.

Phil discussed the *warrior's endurance,* his calling as a man, and his responsibility. Derek reminded Colten of the *warrior's commitment* to study, teach, and coach, and make others successful. Jeff spoke to the *warrior's high character* and being a friend who is not afraid to be accountable and follow through. Gary presented the *warrior as a strategist* who asks questions and analyzes.

Pat explained the *warrior's responsibility to work* and his need to be decisive. Dick discussed the *warrior's leadership,* the need for integrity, and the power of influencing other men. Paul looked at the *warrior's spiritual impact* and how to cultivate a relationship with God and lead men to do the same. Wesley admonished Colten about the *warrior's prayer life* and fighting battles in the spiritual realm.

I discussed the *warrior and his lady*, and Lisa shared about the incredible influence of a godly woman. She presented Colten with a linen handkerchief to place in his Bible as a reminder to pray for his wife. Lisa will present this handkerchief to Colten's wife on their wedding day.

presentation of symbols

"The warrior never serves himself. He is a servant of the king and his commander. Likewise, we must know what and who it is we serve," writes Robert Hicks in *The Masculine Journey.*[4] As part of teaching Colten who he is and who he truly serves, I selected a few symbols of a warrior to give my son during his manhood celebration.

the crest

Together Colten and I designed a copper crest to represent four aspects of who he is and his responsibilities.

The Crown—represents Colten's right to the throne. He is a prince as a child of God.

The Wheat—represents his responsibility to work and manage his domain, and to be fruitful and multiply.

The Sword—represents his role as a warrior to fight with courage, war against evil, and to protect truth and justice.

The Bible and the Cross—represents Colten's need to search the Scriptures diligently for God's Word, the very foundation to his life.

To create this crest, I bought a scrap piece of copper at a metal shop. I traced the four-segmented design in reverse on the backside of the copper. Laying the copper on top of a piece of wood (for the metal to press into) I used a 1/2-inch metal chisel and a hammer to gently and evenly press out the copper. We mounted the finished piece in a wood frame.

the purity ring

As with our daughters, we want our sons to guard their hearts and walk in purity. I asked a jeweler to scan the image of the crest and engrave that image onto a ring. In front of our brothers in Christ, I put this purity ring on Colten's finger to remind him of his pledge to honor and obey God at all costs.

the sword

Leading up to the ceremony, Colten and I together watched select portions of the movie *Braveheart* and discussed how William Wallace laid his life down for his wife and his country. During the ceremony, I presented Colten with a *Braveheart* sword, a replica of the original William Wallace sword.

I purchased the *Braveheart* sword at a specialty shop and had it engraved with William Wallace's words, "Men follow courage, not titles" and the Bible's "Christ did not come to bring peace, but a sword." The immense sword was almost Colten's height. I explained to Colten that although he could not wage war right now with this imposing sword, he would grow into the weight of the sword just as he would grow into the weight of manhood.

The *Brave Heart of a Warrior* ceremony etched an indelible mark on the lives of every man and boy in that room. We all sensed the incredible privilege and responsibility we have to stand courageously as mighty warriors of God calling our sons and their sons to "fight the good fight" (1 Tim. 1:18) for the sake of the cross. We challenge you and your son(s) to fight with us!

personal reflection

❀ What does the Bible say about the role of men and fathers?
❀ How can I begin now to prepare my son for manhood?
❀ What skill do I want my son to conquer as he passes into manhood?
❀ How can we observe my son's passage into manhood?
❀ What men do I want to purposefully influence the heart and mind of my son?

personal prayer

Build me a son, O Lord, who will be strong enough to know when he is weak and brave enough to face himself when he is afraid; one who will be proud and unbending in honest defeat, and humble and gentle in victory.

Build me a son whose wishes will not take the place of deeds; a son who will know Thee—and that to know himself is the foundation stone of knowledge.

Lead him, I pray, not in the path of ease and comfort, but under the stress and spur of difficulties and challenge. Here let him learn to stand up in the storm; here let him learn compassion for those who fail.

Build me a son whose heart will be clear, whose goal will be high; a son who will master himself before he seeks to master other men; one will reach into the future, yet never forget the past.

And after all these things are his, add, I pray, enough of a sense of humor, so that he may always be serious, yet never take himself too seriously. Give him humility, so that he may always remember the simplicity of true greatness, the open mind of true wisdom, and the weakness of true strength.

Then I, his father will dare to whisper, "I have not lived in vain."—General Douglas MacArthur[5]

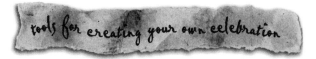

tools for creating your own celebration

Manhood symbols (ring, sword, for example) that are unique to your son
Choose a year in advance a skill your son can finish well
Create a guest list of strong men to speak into your son's life

24

Hearts and Habits of Heroes

> "We cannot rescue America's families unless we make up our minds to save the boys."
> —*William Raspberry*[1]

Working Saturdays as a handyman on a Colorado ranch, I discovered one of life's most treasured rewards—being a mentor to my son. My eight-year-old sidekick probably taught me as much as I taught him on our excursions around the dusty homestead.

Colten proudly handed me tools as we together built porches, dug ditches, and repaired fences. Every step of the way, my son asked questions: "How do you know how to fix this?" "When did the Indians live on this land?" "Do you think heaven will have ranches?"

After about eight months of spending our Saturdays together, we were driving home from the ranch when Colten asked, "Dad, you know why I like coming out here and working with you on Saturdays?"

I could think of dozens of answers to his question, but I said, "No, Colten. Why is that?"

"Because I get all my questions answered."

I took a deep breath, as Colten's answer totally caught me off guard. I pondered the significance of Colten's comments. My son's observation nudged me to realize that I left childhood with so many unanswered questions. My dad was not with me all those years to answer my everyday questions. Those Saturdays alone with Colten gave me hundreds of opportunities to respond to his questions about living life to the fullest. In turn, my son felt loved and secure.

From the time my children turned six, I've made it a habit to take each one out alone to the bagel shop down the street. Over a bagel and hot chocolate, I remind my kids how important they are, and I toss out a few questions: "What are your greatest fears? What are your greatest joys? What are the things that you remember most so far in life?" Together we invite questions and explore answers, delve into struggles and offer solutions. Bit by bit we order the rounded, and sometimes tattered, pieces of life's puzzle.

When we walk away from childhood with unanswered questions, we venture on a winding course of trial and error. Along a bumpy, thorny route in our quest for answers, we burn resources and we burn relationships.

The book *A Fine Young Man* describes this tragic demolition derby for boys: "*The purpose of male adolescence is to activate in the male the ideals of manhood, ideals to which he will commit, by the end of adolescence, to follow the rest of his life.* A boy who learns a set of manhood ideals becomes a man. A boy who does not, wastes his adolescent years, and he will, in some way over the next decades, lay that waste at everyone's feet—in violent behavior; in an inability to fully commit to loved ones; in early death, suicide, or avoidable physical and mental disease; in ongoing self-esteem difficulties; in addictions."[2]

We lose ground whenever we journey through life wondering and doubting. As parents, it's paramount that we invest time in answering the questions of our children. As fathers, we must give our sons a set of manhood ideals that helps them reason and grapple with life's difficult questions.

listening to mentors

I first encountered the idea of someone modeling God-focused manhood to me when I moved to Austin, Texas, at age twenty-two.

Bruce McDonald began to mentor me—he was the first man in my world whom I saw actually live out Christianity. I'd grown up in the church and heard what men were supposed to be, but no man had actively lived his faith up-close before me. For five years, Bruce used the Bible to show me how to live day-by-day in line with God's truth.

After Lisa and I married and started our family, Pat Kelly came alongside me to teach me how to parent children and lead a family. Later Paul Stanley became my leadership mentor honing my skills in guiding and influencing others.

Even before these men, my Uncle Phil Jewett instilled confidence in me to speak and sing in public. He helped me feel comfortable before people. Together these four mentors redirected my priorities and shaped the purpose of my soul. Now I am doing the same for other men and my two sons.

A few years ago, my commitment to proactively mentor my sons spurred me to start a group called *The Hearts and Habits of Heroes*. Michael Gurian says, "We are a monolithic culture with fragments of useful details by which to train our boys to become men, but few fully developed models."[3]

The Hearts and Habits of Heroes seeks to train boys to become men based on biblical models. Once a month, boys ages twelve to fourteen and their dads meet to study a hero of the faith, such as Jonathan Edwards, Abraham Lincoln, or George Mueller. We look for character traits in these noble men that we can draw out and apply in our own lives.

Several of us dads talk to the group about the importance of being courageous warriors and trustworthy leaders who speak the truth, understand our culture, and stand for righteousness. Together we learn to think deeply about God by saturating our minds with theology and memorizing Scripture. We introduce our sons to real-life heroes of conviction and faith.

"Our culture has neglected to see that every boy will make the hero's journey whether we help or not," writes Michael Gurian in *The Wonder of Boys*. "The question is, what kind of hero will he become? If we are intimate teachers who devote our soulful energy to leading that hero through all the possibilities of heroism—from protection to empathy to accomplishment to prayer—the boy will not need to beat up women, join a gang, hate his parents, or destroy his community to be a hero."[4]

What kind of hero do you want *your* boy to become? What kind of heroes are you setting before him?

developing wise habits

What is centered in a hero's heart will reflect in his habits. And a hero's habits can alter the choices of his heart. William Beausay II discusses the need for healthful habits in his insightful book, *Boys!* He writes, "I wanted to summarize and discuss certain patterns of behavior that lead to success. In my observations of winners, it is clear that an '80/20' rule is in effect: 80 percent of the success is created by 20 percent of the habits! The consistent winners are the ones who automatically perform these few behaviors with absolute regularity."[5]

Success is largely linked to consistent habits. Look at Olympic gold medal winners, CEOs of Fortune 500 companies, Nobelprize-winning scientists—all repeat habits of skill and perseverance "with absolute regularity."

Our *Hearts and Habits of Heroes* group is a "university of young sages" who keep notebooks on reading and writing assignments and who learn to articulate truth in a safe circle of fathers and friends. And of course, we always make time each meeting for a game or sports activity.

Hearts and Habits of Heroes also mentors our boys in making sound decisions. William Beausay II notes, "The comedian Gallagher posed this question: 'Why are there floods?' The answer is, 'There are floods because water can make a decision.' If there is one skill deserving of every boy's mastery, it's the skill of good decision making."[6] Good decision making is based on good questions. Some of the questions we need to ask our sons are:

Does this line up with Scripture?

Does this honor God, your parents, and your own personal integrity?

Is this the best use of your gifts and talents?

As fathers, we need to lead our sons into making decisions that protect their hearts and minds and honor God. We need to instill in our boys the sound advice that King Solomon shared with his son, "Make level paths for your feet and take only ways that are firm. Do not swerve to the right or the left; keep your foot from evil. My son, pay attention to my wisdom, listen well to my words of insight, that you may maintain discretion and your lips may preserve knowledge" (Prov. 4:26-5:2).

John Adams, prior to the American Revolution in 1774, exclaimed, "We have not men fit for the times. We are deficient in Genius, in Education, in Gravity, in Fortune, in Everything. I feel unutterable anxiety. God grant us wisdom and fortitude."[7]

John Adams? On the eve of the American Revolution? It seems ludicrous that this man who walked with some of the strongest men in our history would express any signs of inadequacy.

We too may feel deficient at times as men and as fathers; that is why it is helpful to meet regularly with men of like mind. May God grant us all wisdom and fortitude to mentor our sons into discerning, righteous, admirable "men fit for the times."

personal reflection

❀ What or who is shaping my son's thoughts?

✿ How can I proactively build my son's life for his success?

❀ What mentors in the Bible, in history, and in today's world can I introduce my son to?

personal prayer

Lord, thank You for the incredible men in history who walked in power and integrity. May my son never forget the faith that has been passed down to him. Help me and other stalwart men mentor our sons to follow You all the days of their lives. Protect me from pride or fear or anything that could hinder my leading my son into the next generation. Open the eyes of my heart to model sound habits to my sons. Use me to teach him the true knowledge of You. I thank You for the privilege of manhood and fatherhood, and I commit my son and his maturity to You. Amen.

tools for creating your own celebration

Group of spiritually mature male mentors
Group of boys eager to learn from godly men
Place to meet regularly
A notebook to log your *Hearts and Habits* study

PART FOUR

The Gift of Protection

25

Family Foundations

❝Our children are watching us
live, and what we are shouts
louder than anything we can say.**❞**
—Wilferd A. Peterson[1]

Four small children, exhaustion, financial pressures, and adjustments to a new city fueled one of our more memorable arguments. As our frustration with each other escalated, Lisa drove off that Sunday afternoon, and I was left to cool down with the kids. When Lisa returned an hour or so later, the children all eagerly greeted her at the door while I stayed in the kitchen.

"Honey, come here," I calmly called to Lisa.

Not sure what to expect, Lisa slowly stepped into the kitchen as the kids all scrambled to sit at the table. I took Lisa's hand and led her to a chair at the head of the table.

"Honey, please forgive me," I said looking into Lisa's teary eyes. "I'm sorry for my words and actions earlier." I knelt down and with a basin of warm water I began to wash Lisa's feet. Turning to our children excitedly leaning over the edge of the table, I said, "Lauren, Colten, Khrystian, and Jordan, I am here to serve your mom. I am here to protect our family."

That Sunday afternoon I realized more than ever my responsibility to model forgiveness and a serving spirit to my family. One way I serve them is through the Gift of Protection. Our heavenly Father is our all-present Protector, and He gives us specific gifts to protect us: His Word, the Holy Spirit, His armor, wise counsel, truthful words, prayer, and safe dwelling places.

Psalm 91:4-6 declares, "He will cover you with his feathers, and under his wings you will find refuge; his faithfulness will be your shield and rampart. You will not fear the terror of night, nor the arrow that flies by day, nor the pestilence that stalks in the darkness, nor the plague that destroys at midday."

God hides us under the shadow of His wings. We, too, are to gather our children under our "wings" and protect them. In Noah Webster's 1828 dictionary, "protect" means "to cover or shield from danger or injury; to defend; to guard; to preserve in safety."[2]

As parents, we are to safeguard our children from the devouring culture, foolishness, confusion, fear, wrong thinking, and all the rest of Satan's disguised dark schemes. Protection displays indescribable love, value, and honor to our children.

You protect your children as you model purity and righteousness in your life. You shelter your children when you live out Psalm 101:3: "I will set before my eyes no vile thing. The deeds of faithless men I hate; they will not cling to me." You also protect your children when you secure your home as a place of protection, comfort, and safety.

How are you protecting your children's hearts? What words, tones, and example are you setting? How diligently do you keep evil from permeating the walls of your home?

What gifts do you as a parent intentionally want to use to protect your children and generations to come?

battling in prayer

Tim Kimmel, in his noteworthy book *Little House on the Freeway*, describes the touching story of an American soldier fighting in the

Korean War. One night a battle at Heartbreak Ridge raged unusually intense. The North Koreans dug into the mountainous rocks of the ridge, at an advantage over the American and U.N. troops. Flares lit up the night skies and bullets assaulted the air.

One American solider struggled through the maze of enemy installations, but was shot down about fifty meters beyond the enemy's outer lines. He screamed in pain, begging for help. No one moved. A dash to help him was certain suicide. His moans and cries continued—unanswered.

One young man, crouched in a foxhole, kept his head down but kept lifting his wrist up into the light given off by the flares. Suddenly he bolted. Slithering and crawling, he followed the screams until he found his wounded comrade. He grunted and dragged until he was able to pull the solider back through the enemy lines to the safety of an American foxhole.

His sergeant came crawling in to find out what gave him the sudden urge for heroics.

"What in the world got into you?" he asked. "Why did you take that risk?"

"It wasn't really a risk," the young man replied. "I kept checking my watch until I knew it was safe. You see, Sarge, I left on the hour, because it was 9:00 A.M. back home in Kansas. My mom told me before I left that she'd be praying for me every morning at nine o'clock. I knew God would protect me."[3]

Tens of thousands of miles separated that steadfast mom from her solider son hunkered in a muddy foxhole. But prayer connected them to the mercy seat of God. Like this Kansas mom we must pray for the protection of our children. As they fight their way through heated attacks by the Enemy, and someday lonely moments miles from our embrace, we must pray for God to shower them with victory.

foundation of forgivness

The last section of this book shows you how to protect your children through more fun and meaningful *Celebrations of Faith*. In this chapter, we look at the celebrations that build spiritual foundations for your family.

We've written out a family motto: "We are not a perfect family, but we'll always be a forgiving family." We want to cultivate a spirit of forgiveness in our family. When our children get into a fight, we want to jump into that situation as soon as possible and bring understanding and resolution. The key is to clean the slate immediately.

First, as parents we say, "What is the truth here?" Then, we go to our motto: "We're not perfect, but we are a forgiving family," and we ask who needs to ask for forgiveness. Then the child in the wrong looks the offended sibling in the eyes and apologizes with, "Please forgive me for being _____."

This process of teaching our children to forgive takes practice, but it pays incredible rewards for the entire family. Resolving conflict as soon as we can protects each family member from harboring anger and bitterness and giving Satan room to tear apart relationships. For as Ephesians 4:26-27 reminds us, "In your anger do not sin: Do not let the sun go down while you are still angry, and do not give the devil a foothold."

Another aspect of protection for our family is using the Bible as a foundational cornerstone. In the early years of raising our children, we selected a passage of Scripture that we wanted our family to model to each other and the world. As the children have grown, we have memorized these verses together and rely on them in our everyday interactions. We have dedicated Colossians 3:12-17 as the Wilson Family Verses:

> Therefore, as God's chosen people, holy and dearly loved, clothe yourselves with compassion, kindness, humility, gentleness and patience. Bear with each other and forgive whatever grievances you may have against one another. Forgive as the Lord forgave you. And over all these virtues put on love, which binds them all together in perfect unity.
>
> Let the peace of Christ rule in your hearts, since as members of one body you were called to peace. And be

thankful. Let the word of Christ dwell in you richly as you teach and admonish one another with all wisdom, and as you sing psalms, hymns and spiritual songs with gratitude in your hearts to God. And whatever you do, whether in word or deed, do it all in the name of the Lord Jesus, giving thanks to God the Father through him.

How would you summarize your family's mission into a short motto? What Scriptures do you want your children to embrace as the foundation for your family? What verses could you weave into the tapestry of faith you are creating for the generations to come?

We encourage you to write a family motto and select a Bible verse or passage that reflects the purpose and character of your family. You may want to frame your motto and family verse(s) and place the frame in a prominent location in your home as a reminder to "hear God's Word and put it into practice" (Luke 8:21).

personal reflection

❀ What motto could we claim as a family?
✿ What specific Scriptures has God used to encourage our family?
❈ How can I include the kids in selecting a motto and key verse(s) for our family?

personal prayer

Father, may my children learn about relationships and reconciliation and forgiveness and navigating with each other on the basis of Your Word. May our family motto be rooted in each of our hearts to guard our thoughts, words, and actions. Help us to cultivate Your love, Your kindness, Your respect, and Your honor through the Scriptures we claim for our family. Direct our hearts and minds to live in sacred, loving unity with each other. Amen.

tools for creating your own celebration

Bible
Printed motto and Bible verse(s)
Frame to display motto and verse(s)

26

The Blessing Ceremony

> ❝And he took the children
> in his arms, put his hands on
> them and blessed them.❞
> —*Mark 10:16*

"Khrysti, I love your freckles. I love to play with you. You are such a joy," exclaimed three-year-old Colten sitting on the toy box with his tiny hands on his baby sister's head. "I love to play horse with you. God bless you and keep you."

With Colten's last words, two-year-old Khrysti tugged at her diaper and jumped up from the floor swinging her blonde ponytails and shouting, "Tank you!"

What a sight for us to witness! Just the day before we had celebrated our first *Blessing Ceremony* with our family, and our little ones were quick to model my actions. As a couple we had studied about passing on a blessing to our children, but we had no idea what to expect when we decided to make a *Blessing Ceremony* one of our *Celebrations of Faith*.

First, we learned that "blessing" in Hebrew means to speak well of, to invoke a benediction upon someone. In the Greek it means to kneel or lay hands upon. Paul in 2 Timothy 1:6 writes, "I remind you to fan into flame the gift of God, which is in you through the laying on of my hands." In the spiritual realm, the laying on of hands stirs up the gift of God in the person being blessed.

God Himself is the one who initiated a blessing. We read of the world's first blessing ceremony in Genesis 1:28: "God blessed them and said to them, 'Be fruitful and increase in number; fill the earth and subdue it.'"

From the beginning of time, the Lord honored the importance of speaking a blessing to His children. Jehovah blessed Noah after the flood when He promised mankind the covenant of the rainbow (Gen. 9). The patriarchs carried the blessing from generation to generation starting with Abraham in Gensis 12.

In the New Testament we see God the Father bless His Son at His baptism. " 'This is my Son, whom I love; with him I am well pleased'" (Matt. 3:17). Throughout Jesus' ministry, He laid His hands on children and blessed them. "And he took the children in his arms, put his hands on them and blessed them" (Mark 10:16). The last thing the Son of Man did on earth as He ascended into heaven was to bless His disciples.

A blessing in Bible times was significant to a family as we note in the lives of Jacob and Esau. These brothers fought over their father's blessing, which Jacob ended up stealing. Why would Jacob want to steal a blessing—mere words from his father? Isaac did not speak mere words to his oldest son, Esau. As a father, Isaac passed on identity and purpose when he blessed his offspring. A blessing of approval and personal significance can alter the course of not just one child but entire nations!

In their insightful book *The Blessing*, Gary Smalley and John Trent describe five parts of passing on a blessing to someone:

1. **Meaningful touch** (Placing hands on the person.)
2. **Attaching "high value"** ("You bring me great joy." "You are a gifted musician.")
3. **A spoken message** (Describe what you see in the person and why you are proud of him or her.)
4. **Picturing a special future** (A continuation of the

spoken message that says, "I see this in you, therefore . . .")

5. **An active commitment to fulfill the blessing**
    (Setting a consistent time to actually give a blessing.)[1]

the start of a tradition

The first time we gave a blessing to our children, that Sunday afternoon in 1990, Lisa lit a candle in the living room and the kids lined up like a choo-choo train, kneeling from oldest to youngest in front of me in Grandpa Jewett's antique rocker. We all could hardly breathe just soaking in the awe and expectation of what God was about to do in our family.

Taken back by the incredible significance of the moment, I nervously placed my hands on Lauren's head. *Lord, how do I do this? Give me Your words,* I silently prayed.

With tears in my eyes, I looked into Lauren's bright eyes and began to tell her the meaning of her name and how beautiful she was inside and outside. I reminded Lauren that she was a princess of the King and that God would use her in the years ahead to invite others to be a part of His kingdom. I then spoke similar blessings one by one to our other children at the time—Colten, Khrystian, and Jordan.

The next morning Colten excitedly held his own blessing ceremony with little Khyrsti. Not long ago, almost eleven years later, Lisa and I walked into the living room one morning to find four-year-old Logan perched on the piano bench placing his hands on his three-year-old sister, Kameryn, sitting on the floor at his dangling feet. "God bless you, Kammy," Logan proudly commanded his little sister.

All of heaven must watch and smile as our children communicate blessings to their siblings. The joy and pride our children feel when Daddy speaks words of praise and truth into their spirits is beyond words.

Over the years, we've reserved time each Sunday afternoon for our family *Blessing Ceremony*. It's touching to see our littlest ones at the back of the line, eagerly awaiting a blessing from me. Logan stands somber like a brave knight being knighted. After I bless Logan, he wraps his arms around my neck and doesn't want to let go. Little Kameryn does the same thing. Our kids from teen to toddler live for their weekly blessing!

Do your children know how special they are to you? Have you ever received a blessing from someone? You're probably from families like ours, where we never really had a specific ceremony to offer a blessing. You may still be waiting for a blessing from your father. Regardless of your own experience, Your Heavenly Father can add to your life and your children's lives what you may not have received yourself.

help to get you started

You may feel a bit awkward giving a blessing, as I did at first, but God will give you the right words at the right time. To help you pass along a blessing to your children, we've listed the following tips and examples.

> Find out the meaning of your children's names and tell them.
>
> If your children have placed their faith in Christ, tell them that they are princes and princesses of the King.
>
> Look directly into their eyes and tell them that they are beautiful inside and out.
>
> Pick a special character trait they exhibit and tell them God is going to use that special trait to minister to others in the years to come.

You can also use specific Scriptures to communicate a blessing. Here are two examples from Psalm 1:1-3 and Ephesians 1:15-23:

> Blessed is Logan, who does not walk in the counsel of the wicked or stand in the way of sinners or sit in the seat of mockers. But Logan's delight is in the law of the LORD, and on His law Logan meditates day and night. Logan is like a tree planted by streams of water, which yields its fruit in season and whose leaf does not wither. Whatever Logan does prospers.
>
> For this reason, ever since I heard about your faith, Kameryn, in the Lord Jesus and your love for all the saints, I have not

stopped giving thanks for you, Kameryn, remembering you in my prayers. I keep asking that the God of our Lord Jesus Christ, the glorious Father, may give you, Kameryn, the Spirit of wisdom and revelation, so that you may know Him better. I pray also that the eyes of Kameryn's heart may be enlightened in order that she may know the hope to which He has called her, the riches of His glorious inheritance in the saints, and His incomparably great power for Kameryn, who believes.

That power is like the working of His mighty strength, which He exerted in Christ when He raised Him from the dead and seated Him in the heavenly realms, far above all rule and authority, power and dominion, and every title that can be given, not only in the present age but also in the one to come. And God placed all things under His feet and appointed Him to be head over everything for the church, which is His body, the fullness of Him who fills Kameryn in every way.

Another way to bless your sons and daughters is to pray through character qualities from men and women of the Bible:

for daughters

My daughter, you will be like Sarah, loyal and devoted. You will have the courage of Rahab, the prayerful perseverance of Hannah, the gracious wisdom to appeal like Esther, a responsive humble spirit of Mary, the boldness of Anna, the worshipful heart of Mary of Bethany, the hands to serve like Dorcas, and a broken contrite heart of repentance and love for her Savior, a heart fashioned to be the Bride of Christ "all glorious within" (Ps. 45:13, NASB).

for sons

Give my son the wholehearted devotion to keep Your commands as David prayed over Solomon. May he obey God fully like Caleb and have the obedient listening spirit of Samuel. May he be a mighty warrior like Elijah and have the passion of Abraham. May he be a friend of God like Moses, have the tears of Jeremiah, the leadership of Nehemiah, the courage of Stephen, the boldness of Paul, and the servant's heart and love of our Lord and Savior, Jesus Christ.

The story is told of President Adams' son and grandson who went fishing and later wrote in their journals. "Went fishing with my son, waste of time," wrote the father. The son wrote: "Went fishing with my dad, *greatest day of my life*." How do you truly feel about your children? Does giving them a blessing sound like a waste of time?

We encourage you to pass along a blessing to each one of your children. A weekly celebration may not work for you, so try a birthday, family gathering, or when a child accomplishes a certain goal. Every time you communicate a blessing to your children, it will feel not like a waste of time . . . but the greatest day of their lives.

personal reflection

✿ What does it feel like to receive a blessing?
✿ What does God's Word say about blessing others?
✿ How can I consistently impart a blessing to my children?

personal prayer

Elohim, we offer up this sacrifice of blessing to You, for You are the Creator of celebration! Lord God, You blessed Your Son, Jesus, at His baptism with spoken words of love and praise from the heavens. You are the I AM, the same God who blessed Adam and Eve in the world's beginning, and You blessed Noah with a new beginning. You are the same

God who taught patriarchs to bless nations and fathers to bless sons. Jesus, thanks for the example of blessing children when You held little ones on Your lap to bless them.

My family offers up our tiny ceremony of blessing the children and we sense Your pleasure. Lord, I seek to touch my children's hearts with Your love. I desire to magnify their strengths and embrace them with a spiritual mantle of protection through our ceremony of touch and words. Crown my children with Your words of value, dignity, and eternal worth. I join You in saying "blessed are the children." Amen.

tools for creating your own celebration

Time set aside for blessing ceremony
Bible verses to use in offering a blessing
Daddy's Blessing available at your local Christian bookstore or from Cook Communications (see page 223 for more information)

27
The Blessing Journal

> "Nothing has better effect
> upon children than praise."
> —*Sir P. Sidney*[1]

Minutes out of the womb, newborn Logan wailed and screamed, turning his already pinkish body bluish red. Propped on Lisa's chest with our other four kids squirming in excitement around him, little Logan cried like a toddler awakened from a nightmare.

"Logan, son," Randy calmly but firmly said looking into Logan's teary eyes. Immediately Logan's wails stopped. The entire room of nurses and exuberant kids froze in surprised silence. Logan arched his back, turned his head and stared at the man with the soothing voice.

The moment Logan heard his father's voice, his crying ceased. For months this baby boy had heard his family speak to him above his mother's tummy. Now hearing the voice of his dad, perhaps Logan felt protected and safe—with no need to cry. Randy continued Logan's first blessing by anointing him with oil and speaking the meaning of his name, "man of honor." Logan had heard these words of blessing for nine months in the womb. We believe he knew his father's voice.

Photos from Logan's first blessing adorn the inside cover of his *Blessing Journal*, a collection of written prayers and words of praise by us, his parents. Lisa has glued photos of each child's first *Blessing Ceremony* in a lined journal. A *Blessing Journal* is a simple way we record words of encouragement, value, and praise for our children.

We may not have thick baby books for each of our kids, but as they each leave home, they'll take a *Blessing Journal* with twenty-some years of our personal prayers for them. The very first thing God did after creating Adam and Eve was to bless them. If only we had photos of that momentous occasion!

One prayer of thanksgiving that's written in Jordan's *Blessing Journal* describes the Sunday afternoon after her Daddy blessed her and she crawled into her mom's lap and exclaimed, "Momma, Daddy is just like Jesus when he blesses me."

Do your children see Jesus in your life? Do you speak words of grace and affirmation to them? The *Blessing Ceremony* and *Blessing Journal* are easy ways to touch your family with God's beauty and power. The power of the written word that they can read the rest of their lives is an indispensable gift!

It only takes a few minutes to write out the strengths you see in your kids, the joy they bring to your family. Yet God will take those few minutes and multiply them into years and years of encouragement, hope, and comfort for each of your children, who will in turn do the same for their children. What a legacy of blessings you can start by picking up a pen today!

personal reflection

❧ How have others encouraged me with written affirmations?
❧ What does the Bible say about encouraging others?
❧ What three things can I praise each of my children for today?

personal prayer

Almighty God, may these written words of blessing delight the hearts of my children and descendants for generations. Take each word and inscribe into the minds and souls of my children my devoted love for them. Help us as a family weave a marvelous legacy of blessings for the entire world to know that You alone are our blessed Redeemer. I praise You for creating my children. I praise You for blessing us with Your love and protection. In Jesus' name, amen.

tools for creating your own celebration

Journal or notebook
Photos of a child's blessing ceremony or joyful family
 photo
Glue or photo corners

28

Celebrate the Truth

> **“**Life consists of what a person thinks about all day.**”**
> —*Emerson*[1]

Eight-year-old Lauren stumbled hurriedly up the stairs to our bedroom. "Mommy, Mommy! There's thoughts in my head!" she blurted, gasping for breath.

"Sweetheart, what are you talking about?" Lisa gently asked.

"There's thoughts in my head and these thoughts are telling me I don't worship the true God," Lauren cried, burying her head in Lisa's side.

We were dumbfounded by Lauren's words, but we reassured her that those thoughts were not true and were coming from Satan. "But the thoughts . . . the thoughts told me not to tell my parents!" Lauren continued, trying to choke back her fear.

After calming Lauren down, Randy walked Lauren to her room where he anointed Lauren and her room with oil and boldly prayed that Satan would flee and remove himself from Lauren's thoughts. He prayed that Lauren would put on the armor of God and rest assured that she was in Christ. Immediately God's peace embraced Lauren and the troubling doubts about her loyalty to God vanished.

A friend later told us that almost the exact same thoughts came to him when he was about Lauren's age, but he fearfully obeyed the "don't tell your parents" command reverberating in his head. For the next twenty-five years or so, our friend lived fearing that he did not worship the true God. In full-time Christian ministry, he finally attended a conference and learned how to free himself from the bondage of Satan's lies. This could have been Lauren's plight had she not come to us, and we wielded God's truth against Satan's lies. One thought can paralyze a life!

thinking biblically

In the next few chapters we will look at *Celebrations of Faith* that help our children think biblically, speak biblically, and act biblically. To think biblically means to tell ourselves the truth. Teaching our children to stand in God's Truth is one of the most stable gifts of protection we can offer. Lies are not so much a *dismissal* of the truth, but a *distortion* of the truth. We see the Enemy first hissing out his distortions in the Garden of Eden with "Did God really say . . . ?"

Since man first walked on the earth, Satan has connived and coerced to infest human minds with doubts and lies. But God does not leave us weak-willed defenseless pawns—His Word and His Spirit crush the Father of Lies and his deceitful tactics. Take a look at God's arsenal in Ephesians 6:10-17:

> Finally, be strong in the Lord and in his mighty power. Put on the full armor of God so that you can take your stand against the devil's schemes. For our struggle is not against flesh and blood, but against the rulers, against the authorities, against the powers of this dark world and against the spiritual forces of evil in the heavenly realms. Therefore put on the full armor of God, so that when the day of evil comes, you may be able to stand your ground, and after you have done everything, to stand. Stand firm then, with the belt of truth buckled around your waist, with the breastplate of righteousness in place, and with your feet fitted with the readiness that comes from the gospel

of peace. In addition to all this, take up the shield of faith, with which you can extinguish all the flaming arrows of the evil one. Take the helmet of salvation and the sword of the Spirit, which is the word of God.

God wraps us "with the belt of truth" (verse 14) to counter the Enemy's lies. As parents, we aim to teach our children who they are in Christ and how they can protect themselves with His truth. We practice *Celebrate Truth* to protect our children's spirits.

One of the key aspects of thinking the truth of God is to gain control of your thoughts. Proverbs 16:3 says, "Commit thy works unto the LORD, and thy thoughts shall be established" (KJV). As we commit our everyday lives and work to God, in the spiritual realm He literally establishes our thoughts.

In *Hung By the Tongue* Francis P. Martin writes, "Thoughts are the original ideas. Imaginations are the image, and strongholds are a result of thoughts that come to reality. The stronghold is what controls you if you allow it to. Jesus has given you authority over your thinking, but you have to take authority and stay in authority. It is an act of your will. An imagination is an intent to do something about what you've been thinking, and a stronghold is when the choice is not yours anymore, but you have submitted your will to the thought."[2]

We have further admonition from 2 Corinthians 10:5 to "take captive every thought to make it obedient to Christ." Elisabeth Elliot has said in one of her messages, "Taking thoughts captive is not a gentle business." But as Philippians 2:13 reminds us "for it is God who is at work in you." God Himself gives us the discernment and strength to reign in our thoughts.

knowing who we are

"The number one influence on children is their concept of the truth," says speaker and author Josh McDowell. "They are 600 percent more likely to commit suicide if *they* are the center of truth."[4] The world thrives on telling our children that truth revolves around them.

Why follow God when you can self-actualize your own destiny?

This is why it's crucial that we understand who we really are in God's eyes. It's been said that "fear makes us smaller than we are," and when the ten spies returned from their reconnaissance mission to the Promised Land, they conceded, "We seemed like grasshoppers in our own eyes, and we looked the same to them" (Num. 13:33).

How we see ourselves in our eyes is how others will see us. Proverbs 23:7 (NASB) states, "For as he thinks within himself, so he is." How do you view yourself? How do your children view themselves? Are you believing lies about yourselves or God's truth?

Over the years we have developed the following truth versus lies principles that we review with our children. We pray that these points will help your family take your thoughts captive in the reality of God's Word.

self-lies	truth
I just can't help it when I fail.	And God is able to make all grace abound to you, so that in all things at all times, having all that you need, you will abound in every good work (2 Cor. 9:8).
I always feel defeated, so I must be.	But thanks be to God! He gives us the victory through our Lord Jesus Christ (1 Cor. 15:57).
I feel so paralyzed by fear at times.	For God did not give us a spirit of timidity, but a spirit of power, of love and of self-discipline (2 Tim. 1:7).

I see no results in my day-to-day life when I walk in the truth.	The righteous will live by faith (Gal. 3:11).
I'll never change; I'll always fail.	The Lord will accomplish what concerns me (Ps. 138:8 NASB).
I'm so weary. I just don't have the strength to go on.	The way of the Lord is strength to the upright (Prov. 10:29 KJV).
I'm just not capable to do this task, even though God has called me to it.	I can do everything through him who gives me strength (Phil. 4:13).
I blew it again! How can God possibly keep forgiving me?	If we confess our sins, he is faithful and just and will forgive us our sins and purify us from all unrighteousness (1 John 1:9).
I'm so worthless. I feel so stupid.	Then God said, "Let us make man in our image, in our likeness. . . . So God created man in his own image (Genesis 1: 26-27).
	Can a mother forget the baby at her breast and have no compassion on the child she has borne? Though she may forget, I will not forget you! See, I have engraved you on the palms of my hands. (Isa. 49:15-16).
I feel so overwhelmed at times. I just feel like I'm losing my mind.	You will keep in perfect peace him whose mind is steadfast, because he trusts in you (Isa. 26:3).

I quit. No one even cares about all I do for God anyway.

Be steadfast, immovable, always abounding in the work of the Lord, knowing that your toil is not in vain in the Lord (1 Cor. 15:58 NASB).

I can't be used by God unless I'm strong.

"My grace is sufficient for you, for my power is made perfect in weakness." Therefore I will boast all the more gladly about my weaknesses, so that Christ's power may rest on me (2 Cor. 12:9).

I have to be perfect to be accepted.

If we claim to be without sin, we deceive ourselves and the truth is not in us (1 John 1:8).

I need everyone's approval in my life.

Whatever you do, work at it with all your heart, as working for the Lord, not for men, since you know that you will receive an inheritance from the Lord as a reward. It is the Lord Christ you are serving (Col. 3:23-24).

Am I now trying to win the approval of men, or of God? Or am I trying to please men? If I were still trying to please men, I would not be a servant of Christ (Gal. 1:10).

Life should be easy.	In this world you will have trouble. But take heart! I have overcome the world (John 16:33).
I still feel so sinful, even after I ask forgiveness. I must not be sincere enough.	Therefore, there is now no condemnation for those who are in Christ Jesus (Rom. 8:1).
I deserve to strive for happiness in my life and get it.	Whoever finds his life will lose it, and whoever loses his life for my sake will find it (Matt. 10:39).

Can you relate to some of these common lies? If so, why not make it a habit to meditate and even memorize the truthful verses of God's Word? We encourage you also to sit down with your children and talk through the healthy and unhealthy thoughts that they encounter day by day. Together as a family you can thwart Satan's lies and live out the power of John 8:32: "Then you will know the truth, and the truth will set you free."

personal reflection

❀ What do I believe to be true about God?

❀ What do I believe about God that isn't true?

❀ How are Satan's lies affecting my children?

❀ As I observe my children, what lies do they seem to fight the most?

❀ How can we as a family practice taking our thoughts captive for Christ?

personal prayer

Father, I commit to be a truth seeker and a lover of the truth in every way. I pray that my family would ground everything in the power and authority of the Scriptures in our lives. Fill my children with the knowledge of You, that they would take every thought and purpose captive in obedience to Christ. May my children's minds be engulfed in the presence of the Author and Finisher of their faith.

Help each of us to only believe that which is true, worthy, honorable, just, pure, lovely, and gracious. If there is any virtue of excellence or anything worthy of praise, may we as a family think on these things. Guard us from speculations or vain imaginations that would destroy the truth that has been planted and watered by the Spirit of God in our lives. As a parent, I commit to protecting the truth, speaking the truth, and living the truth at all costs in my thoughts and in my home on a daily basis. In Jesus' holy name, amen.

tools for creating your own celebration

. Bible

29

Words of Life

> **"**The quickest and surest way toward thoughtfulness is the tongue—use it for the good of others. If you think well of others, you will also speak well of others. Violence of the tongue is very real—sharper than any knife, wounding and creating bitterness that only the grace of God can heal.**"**
> —*Mother Teresa*[1]

Standing at the kitchen sink, I clenched my teeth and hunched up my shoulders in utter agony. Ear-rattling, shrill, high notes floated from the mouths of my four oldest children. Each exuberant child spun around in the kitchen belting out a separate song. Four melodies, four off-beat rhythms, four over-zealous performers.

Finally at the edge of my wits, I yelled, "Stop singing!"

Silence engulfed the room. I'll never forget the stunned look on my children's faces. So absorbed in their joyful choruses, they had no idea they were all singing different tunes. And I'll never forget God's whisper to me that morning: "Lisa, do you really want your children to remember you shouting, 'Stop singing'? *Let the children sing.*"

I quickly apologized to my children, and with God's admonition, let the children sing. Yet my brusque words that day in the kitchen shot endless echoes into my soul. Words hurt and words heal.

The Bible speaks volumes on the importance of our words. Proverbs 18:21 warns us, "The tongue has the power of life and death." One of our family's celebrations is *Words of Life* that remind us to speak biblically by replacing words of death with words of life. Let's take a quick look at the effect of our words as recorded in the Book of Proverbs.

> *The tongue has the power of life and death,*
> *and those who love it will eat its fruit.*
> *—Proverbs 18:21*

words of life

A word aptly spoken is like apples of gold in settings of silver (Prov. 25:11).

A gentle tongue can break a bone (25:15).

Perfume and incense bring joy to the heart, and the pleasantness of one's friend springs from his earnest counsel (27:9).

Wounds from a friend can be trusted, but an enemy multiplies kisses (27:6, NKJV).

He who rebukes a man will in the end gain more favor than he who has a flattering tongue (28:23).

A wise man's heart guides his mouth, and his lips promote instruction (16:23).

words of death

As a north wind brings rain, so a sly tongue brings angry looks (Prov. 25:23).

Like a city whose walls are broken down is a man who lacks self-control (25:28).

Do not answer a fool according to his folly, or you will be like him yourself. Answer a fool according to his folly, or he will be wise in his own eyes (26:4-5).

The words of a gossip are like choice morsels; they go down to a man's inmost parts (26:22).

A malicious man disguises himself with his lips, but in his heart he harbors deceit. Though his speech is charming, do not believe him (26:24-25).

From the fruit of his mouth a man's stomach is filled; with the harvest of his lips he is satisfied (18:20).

It is to a man's honor to avoid strife, but every fool is quick to quarrel (20:3).

Pleasant words are a honeycomb, sweet to the soul and healing to the bones (16:24).

The tongue of the righteous is choice silver. . . . The lips of the righteous nourish many (10:20-21).

He who refreshes others will himself be refreshed (11:25).

From the fruit of his lips a man is filled with good things (12:14).

Truthful lips endure forever, but a lying tongue lasts only a moment (12:19).

From the fruit of his lips a man enjoys good things (13:2).

He who guards his lips guards his soul, but he who speaks rashly will come to ruin (13:3).

The tongue that brings healing is a tree of life, but a deceitful tongue crushes the spirit (15:4).

A lying tongue hates those it hurts, and a flattering mouth works ruin (26:28).

Do you see a man who speaks in haste? There is more hope for a fool than for him (29:20).

He who answers before listening— that is his folly and his shame (18:13).

An angry man stirs up dissension, and a hot-tempered one commits many sins (29:22).

It is a trap for a man to dedicate something rashly and only later to consider his vows (20:25).

Put away perversity from your mouth; keep corrupt talk far from your lips (4:24).

When words are many, sin is not absent, but he who holds his tongue is wise (10:19).

With his mouth the godless destroys his neighbor, but through knowledge the righteous escape (11:9).

The teaching of the wise is a fountain of life, turning a man from the snares of death (13:14).

A gentle answer turns away wrath, but a harsh word stirs up anger (15:1).

The tongue of the wise commends knowledge, but the mouth of the fool gushes folly (15:2).

A fool shows his annoyance at once, but a prudent man overlooks an insult (12:16).

A man who lacks judgment derides his neighbor, but a man of understanding holds his tongue. A gossip betrays a confidence, but a trustworthy man keeps a secret (11:12-13).

The words of the wicked lie in wait for blood, but the speech of the upright rescues them (12:6).

Reckless words pierce like a sword, but the tongue of the wise brings healing (12:18).

Psalm 34:12-13 instructs us, "Whoever of you loves life and desires to see many good days, *keep your tongue from evil and your lips from speaking lies.*" We want our children to understand that their speech can foster harm or health. Sarcasm and complaining are two negative word habits that lead to death.

In Greek the word sarcasm literally means "tearing flesh." If we use sarcasm in the home, our caustic words rip at the hearts of our children and shred apart who they are.

Behavioral researcher Shad Helmstetter points out in his book *Choice* that complaining creates a negative programming process in the brain and releases destructive chemicals in the body. Helmstetter writes:

And if an individual who has not yet learned that complaining— or not complaining—is a choice, spent no more than fifteen minutes a day causing himself or herself to complain or be upset about the normal difficulties of the day, those few minutes of self-imposed aggravation would add up to *more than 5,000 irreplaceable minutes* of powerfully negative self-programs in just one year.[2]

We must teach ourselves and our children that we control the choice to complain or not complain. Losing five thousand minutes a year to complaining is a somber waste of God's gift of time.

Proverbs 16:23 exhorts, "A wise man's heart guides his mouth, and his lips promote instruction." How do our hearts guide our mouths? What are we teaching with our lips?

teaching words of life

One way we use words to elevate our children's minds and hearts is through the *Wilson Family Words of Life*. We had a family meeting, and the children helped us choose words that made them feel loved and valued. We've inscribed these words on a poster that hangs in our kitchen for all to view and meditate upon regularly.

Wilson Family Words of Life

"The tongue that brings healing is a tree of life." (Prov.15:4).
"Take to heart all the words I have solemnly declared to you this day, so that you may command your children to obey carefully all the words of this law. They are not just idle words for you—they are your life" (Deut. 32:46-47).

I love you. • I will *always* love you! • *God* loves you. • You are fully accepted and unconditionally loved in this family, now and always. • I am sorry, please forgive me. • I *forgive you.* • You are doing a *great* job! • I'm *so* proud of you, I *knew* you could do it! • You bring so much joy to our home. • You are a prince/princess of the King! • You are a blessing. • You are such a servant. • You are very important. • You are an incredible gift. • You are *precious.* • You are created *exactly* the way God wanted you! • I see God's image in you. • God made you with so many talents. • You are our *treasure!* • We are champions. • We expect the best. • We persevere. • We never quit. • I'm here to serve you and make you a success. • We need you in this family. • Our family would not be the same without you!

Underneath our *Words of Life*, we've included our family motto: "We are not a perfect family, but we will always be a forgiving family." We've also listed each child's name and his or her God-given strengths. Our kids love seeing this poster every day!

Words give life to our very souls. What words frame the reputation of your family? Are your words built on Scripture?

We're teaching our children not to use words to fight but to answer words with the truth of God. Proverbs 26:4 says: "Do not answer a fool according to his folly, or you will be like him yourself." When we retaliate with words we become like our verbal attacker.

We sat down with our kids and said, "What words do you want to hear that make you feel loved? What words bring you life?" We wrote down these loving words and our children's strengths. When our children get in an argument with each other, they are to ask for forgiveness and refer to this list.

After reconciliation comes the *restoration of honor*. Choosing kind words about the other person's strengths replaces the hurtful words of death. We must break any spoken curses and replace them with words of blessing, restoring honor to each other. This, of course, takes lots of practice, but we are seeing fewer careless words tossed around in our home.

speaking words of blessing

We also bless each other with our words using a concept based on Florence Littauer's book *Silver Boxes*. Over the years we've collected a variety of silver boxes—some ornate jewelry boxes, some simple curio boxes—and placed them around our home. Whenever one of us feels in need of a blessing or wants to build up another, he or she will pass a silver box to someone. This person then speaks words of life to the others present.

We regularly pass a silver box around at the dinner table to teach the children to express words of kindness to each other. If we don't cultivate the habit of our children blessing each other, they won't. We, the parents, must share our children's love for each other by capturing a moment to speak beauty to each other.

When people who don't know the Lord witness these verbal affirmations in our home, they often weep—words of life pierce deeply into our souls. For as Mother Teresa once said, "Kind words can be short and easy to speak, but their echoes are truly endless."[3] We often give silver boxes as birthday and Christmas gifts with a note, "Bless each other. Cultivate words of life."

After we gave our friend Laurie a silver box for her birthday, she began to incorporate the silver box blessings into family birthdays. Offering words of blessing to each other was initially quite a challenge for her three boys. Now she says, "Sometimes, our blessings are just a simple: 'I think you're a great baseball player, Matt,' or 'I really like the way you always play with me and include me when your friends are over.' These words are not only a blessing to the birthday boy, but definitely ones to fill a mother's soul. After hearing three very competitive boys compete with each other every day, all day, the positive words are water to my parched soul."

Another fun yet simple way we pass along kind words is by writing encouraging notes with dry-erase markers on the mirrors in our house or in our cars. A quickly scribbled, "I love you," "You're special," or "I'm proud of you" does wonders for your spirit. At Christmas we put written blessings into silver Christmas ornaments that open up. We read the blessings to each other before we open our gifts.

celebrating courtesy

Aristotle once said, "We are what we repeatedly do. Excellence, then, is not an act, but a habit."[4] Another habit we want to teach our children is to celebrate courtesy. Manners are a powerful way of giving respect to each other. Manners set a tone of honor in our homes. Manners elevate servanthood and self-control and teach us to place others above ourselves. Titus 3:2 encourages us to, "be peaceable and considerate, and to show true humility toward all men."

Courtesy crowns others with royalty by presenting them the gift of blessing and value. "Instilling poise is a vital part of a legacy of love. . . . Parents leave a legacy of love to their children when they transfer skills that make the most of moments and relation-ships," writes Tim Kimmel in *Raising Kids Who Turn Out Right*. "Regardless of our economic background, we need to equip our children to hobnob with hoboes and highbrows with equal ease. Whether they are having duck flambé with the homeless or flipping hamburgers on the hibachi with [a princess], we need to pass on to them refinements that will allow them to move into any situation with confidence."[5] Here are some specific courtesy guidelines we've set up to bring order in our home and instill poise and confidence in our children.

morning manners

1. Awake, greet each other with a smile and hug and say, "This is the day that the Lord has made, I will rejoice and be glad in it."
2. Use quiet, cheerful, and respectful voices.
3. Help each other with breakfast duties until everything is finished.
4. Respect each other's "space" by keeping your beds made and rooms clean before school.

speaking manners

1. Always answer "yes, ma'am" or "yes, sir" and look into the eyes of adults when they ask you a question.
2. Upon meeting a new adult or child, smile, extend your hand and say, "Hi, I'm _____. It's so good to meet you."
3. When speaking, lift your head and speak loud enough to be understood.
4. If you don't understand a command or statement, say "Pardon me, could you repeat that?"

phone manners

1. When answering the phone, use a cheerful tone and say, "Hello, Wilsons', may I please ask who's calling?"
2. Listen carefully and then say, "Just a minute, please." Then repeat to Mom or Dad exactly what was said.
3. If taking a message, speak clearly and loudly to ask any questions you need answered or repeated. Then write the message down.
4. Do not yell for Mom or Dad. Come and get us, speaking quietly.
5. Do not come to Mom or Dad with questions while we are speaking on the phone, unless it's an emergency.

table manners

1. Cheerfully set the table.
2. Wash hands and brush hair before every meal.
3. Stand at the table until Mom or hostess is seated or says you may sit.
4. Do not take a bite until after prayer and until Mom, Dad, or hostess begins to eat.
5. When passing food, ask "May I please have the _____. Thank you. You're welcome."
6. Stay seated until all are finished.
7. After the meal is finished, ask Mom or the hostess, "Thank you for the good meal; may I please be excused?" Then clear your plate and rinse it.

guest manners

1. When a guest arrives, always try to greet him or her at the door with a smile or hug and say you're glad to have this person visit.

2. Always ask first, "What would you like to play today?"
3. Make your guest feel special by sharing your toys and games.
4. Always include your brothers and sisters and value them by playing with them along with your guest.
5. Always offer your guest a snack or drink before you have one.
6. When you're the guest at someone's home never ask for a snack unless it is offered to you first and only ask for water if you need a drink.

respect manners

1. If you've wronged someone, go to him or her with a hug, look in the person's eyes and say, "I'm sorry for _____, please forgive me." The other person needs to hug back and say "I forgive you."
2. Use self-control by waiting and not interrupting when someone else is speaking and you have a question.
3. Make others feel valued and important by being good listeners and asking lots of good questions. This will make you wise as well!
4. To keep order, each of you is responsible to pick up your things when you've used them.
5. Always hold the door for everyone who is coming in behind you.
6. We will rejoice when one rejoices and weep when one is hurt, loving each other with sensitivity. (Courtesy of the heart by God.)

We are daily working to teach our children to honor each other in our home. We, like you, have good days and bad days, but we can always start over with a new day. Celebrating courtesy cultivates life in the spirit. We encourage you to design your own family manners that will bless each of you and all your guests.

calming words of love

One Sunday during a worship service, our three-year-old Logan and two-year-old Kameryn were unusually fussy during the opening music. While the rest of us delighted in the worship songs, Randy sat down and drew Logan close. With his arms around Logan, Randy began to whisper in his ear, "Logan, you are our man of honor. I love you and I'm proud of you." Almost immediately our unsettled little boy settled calmly on Randy's lap.

Next Randy pulled Kameryn from circling her mother's legs and drew her into his arms. He whispered in her ear, "Honey, you are our beloved one. You are beautiful and I love you." Within a minute, our rambunctious daughter snuggled into her daddy's lap next to Logan. Together the two of them rested contentedly for the next hour.

The week leading up to that Sunday our family schedule was extra hectic, and our little ones especially experienced the fallout. Their fussing and whining showed us they lacked our attention. But instead of hurling harsh words at them, Randy's decision to speak loving, truthful thoughts into their little ears calmed their behavior and soothed their spirits.

We truly have a choice with the words of our tongue. Our lips can bless or our lips can curse. Luke 6:28 admonishes us to "bless those who curse you, pray for those who mistreat you." God further reminds us in, 1 Peter 3:8-11:

> Finally, all of you, live in harmony with one another; be sympathetic, love as brothers, be compassionate and humble. Do not repay evil with evil or insult with insult, but with blessing, because to this you were called so that you may inherit a blessing. For, "Whoever would love life and see good days must keep his tongue from evil and his lips from deceitful speech. He must turn from evil and do good; he must seek peace and pursue it."

Are you teaching your children to turn the other cheek? Are you showing them how to "seek peace and pursue it"? As the Book of James advises us, the tongue is so small yet so mighty in its effect. Only by placing our tongues under God's control can we offer words of life to others. We all slip up now and then, but developing speech that graces others with love, respect, and good things, enriches our own body and soul. May we all weave words of life into the heart and spirit of our children not just for today, but for generations to come.

In *Silver Boxes*, Florence Littauer shares the story of her mother-in-law's final days in a nursing home. Mother Littauer in her early years aspired to sing professionally, but did not receive encouragement from loved ones to pursue her dream. She chose marriage and motherhood, and now near the end of her life, she could no longer recognize her family. Her once sharp mind seemed disconnected from her body. Florence Littauer describes a visit to see her beautiful but silent mother-in-law:

> I asked the nurse who cared for her, "Does Mother ever talk?"
>
> She replied, "Oh no, she never says a word."
>
> As we discussed the tragedy of a once brilliant mind gone dead, the nurse made an interesting comment, "It's the strangest thing. She can't talk, but every so often she sings opera."
>
> The nurse, who knew nothing of Mother's repressed desires, marveled at how she could stand and sing when she couldn't say a word. Isn't it amazing that those unfulfilled dreams are stamped so indelibly in our minds that even when all else is lost, those memories are not erased?
>
> The night before Mother died, the nurse later told us, she stood by her chair after dinner and began to sing. She put on a moving performance and the nurse clapped in approval as Mother bowed and smiled. The next morning when the nurse went in, Mother was lying with her hands folded across her chest and with a smile on her face. She had sung her last song on earth and had been applauded by the angels.
>
> Mother had talent that was never developed, a music box that was never allowed to play, a career that was never begun.
>
> Mother died with the music still in her.[6]

Will your children die with the music still in them? Let's pray that our children will die singing all the music they were created to sing. Let the children sing!

What words do my children need to hear to feel loved?

What bad habits of the tongue has my family developed?

What "course of life" has my tongue set on fire?

How are we doing in reconciling and restoring honor?

Father, help us choose words of life in our family. Help us speak and meditate on words that reveal the reputation and character of our home for future generations. Literally bind words of truth, grace, and kindness in our hearts and reflect them in our actions. I choose life today, that my children may live. I choose words that speak to my children's beautiful and fragile spirits.

Together we choose life in the way we conduct ourselves and the tone we use with each other. We choose forgiveness and reconciliation. May we choose to humble ourselves before each other and let Your cleansing blood restore our relationships. Guard our lips from speaking death. Use me to shape the boundaries of truth and beauty in my children's hearts and lives. Lord, I commit who we are and what we say to You in Jesus' name. May our family words of life pave the way for Your love in our children and our children's children. Amen.

30

Family Covenant

"Covenant is all about communion with another. Its purpose is to offer us a lifelong opportunity to be deeply known."
—Daniel A. Brown[1]

The floor quaked with each heaving sob of the hefty six-foot-five-inch man. Some may say grown men don't cry, but this stalwart man sat in the auditorium weeping over our message on making a covenant to protect our children.

A farmer and a father of thirteen, this dad was broken by his failure to be more of a godly leader to his family. Yet our words encouraged him to take small steps toward change. That day he made a promise to God to take a more active stand in guarding his time and his family.

About five years ago, we, too, made a significant promise to God. Together we wrote a *Wilson Family Covenant* that pledges us as parents to care for, protect, and teach our children in the ways of the Lord. We typed out our covenant as a document that can literally be passed down for generations.

We invited one of our mentor couples over for a formal ceremony of signing our covenant before our children. Randy got on his knees and washed each of the children's feet and told them how we promise to be there to serve them, nurture them, and shelter them through life. "Kids, I'm going to lead you because I'm going to serve you," vowed Randy. "I'm here to show you Jesus Christ."

We also gave each child a metal ID bracelet with his or her name engraved on the front and "Covenant of Love" and the date engraved on the back. Because the Bible talks of breaking bread as a sign of a covenant, we broke a loaf of homemade bread as a sign of our family covenant.

Our mentors gave brief testimonies of how they came to faith in Christ and signed the document as witnesses to our pledge. Our children individually told how they too had accepted Jesus as their Savior. The kids were all dressed up, and just beamed at our celebration of our commitment to them.

As parents we wanted to be held accountable for the spiritual boundaries of our children. Our framed family covenant hangs on our living room wall as a continual reminder of our promise. We've included a copy of our family covenant to help you tailor a document for your family.

Wilson Family Covenant

We promise to teach you the laws and statutes of the Lord that will provide for you and protect you.

We promise to nurture you in the teaching and admonition of the Lord when you rise up, walk in the way, and lie down.

We promise to provide for you a gentle, holy sanctuary in our home in which you can hear God and learn to love Him and walk with Him.

We promise to protect you from physical,

emotional, mental, and spiritual trauma within the safety net of your family.

We promise to "narrow" your way as the Hebrew word for "train up" means. We will set and reinforce boundaries, which will show you God's love and our love and thus give you freedom.

We promise to reinforce our family motto daily, "We are not a perfect family, but we will always be a forgiving family."

We promise to ask your forgiveness when we have failed you and seek reconciliation with you and with God.

We promise to constantly ask each other "what is the truth" to help us refocus on our God and His plan for us in the midst of difficult circumstances.

We promise to diligently pass on what your grandmothers and grandfathers for generations have passed on to us—the legacy of truth.

We promise to remember and repeat God's great goodness and provision for us, so that we will always remain humbly grateful for the great things He has done.

We promise to constantly seek to know each of you intimately, as God seeks to reveal Himself to us. We'll seek to ask God to show us your bents as He created you, your strengths, weaknesses, and talents. And we will offer them up to God as a holy sacrifice unto Him.

We promise to continue our traditions of new celebrations of faith God brings to us—celebrations which will tie our heartstrings to the truth and set up markers of remembrance to our God and to you.

All these promises of our family covenant we make to you, our children, Lauren, Colten, Khrystian, Jordan, Logan, and Kameryn, before our most Holy God, and we seek His grace and counsel in our lives to enable us to purposefully carry out this covenant

on this____ day of_____ (month)_____ (year)
Signed _____
Witnesses_____
_____

Our dear mentors Paul and Phyllis witnessed our *Family Covenant* celebration. Phyllis describes their part in our ceremony:

Randy and Lisa have included my husband, Paul, and me in so many of their significant family events. When they dedicated their *Family Covenant* to the Lord, we watched the children gather around their father as he taught them the principles of the covenant and the high standards to which they would commit themselves as a family.

Randy spoke words of blessing to each of his children as he laid hands on them and then washed each of their feet. Lisa helps Randy by creating an atmosphere of warmth and encourages her children to value the strength and protection of their dad. After reading the words of the covenant, Paul and I signed the covenant as witnesses of this sacred event, committing ourselves to pray for this precious family. We wish that every family could experience such a presence of God.

We encourage you to make a written pledge of protection to your children and celebrate your vows with a special ceremony. Your children will never forget this momentous occasion!

❋ How serious am I about a commitment to protect and provide spiritually for my family?

❋ What does God's Word says about covenants?

❋ What promises am I willing to make to my family?

Father, we commit our family covenant to You. We commit the spiritual boundaries that we have chosen for the lives of our children and our grandchildren. Father, we do not take this covenant lightly. We take it seriously, before the throne of God, that it is a place of authority that our children will take and receive and take into their new families when they leave our home, that it is a place of beauty, a place of love, and a place where we have invited Your Spirit to come in and to seal our words and promises before You this day.

Father, we pray that the Enemy would have no ground to come in and change the boundaries that we've set before You. We pray that as it is done on earth, it will be done in heaven, and that You would take the words that we have written and create a place of holiness, authority, and redemption for all of the generations to come, and we humbly present this document, this covenant, before You on this day, and we pray that in your power, He who has begun it will complete it in the name of Jesus.

31

Choose Life!

> 66 God Himself is interested in birthing
> and maturing deep relationships between
> people that can speak to and affect those
> around them, and can continue to speak
> for generations and into eternity itself. 99
> —*James Lucas*[1]

Hunger pains diverted the course of world history. Genesis 27 tells us Isaac's twin son Esau tossed away his birthright for a helping of lentil stew. Esau's compulsive action pumped rippling waves of selfishness, greed, and immorality into his bloodline. This hairy man's demand to satisfy his hunger led to spiritual starvation for generations of his ancestors. Let's look at Esau's twisted legacy lived out centuries later in the Herod family.[2]

Herod the Great was an Edomite, a descendent of red-skinned Esau (Edom means "red" in Hebrew). Esau and his descendants were cursed because they hated the things of God. As desert marauders who lived by the sword (Gen. 27:40), the Edomites pestered the Jewish people.

Herod the Great is not fully an Edomite, he is also half Jewish, which is a picture of man's war within between good and evil. In spite of Herod's tarnished ancestry, God mercifully presents Herod with the opportunity to choose good and break the generational curse passed down to him.

In Matthew 2:1-3, we read that the wise men approach Herod the Great, king over Judea. The magi ask the king, "Where is the one who has been born king of the Jews?" The words of the foreigners greatly disturb Herod. God is knocking on King Herod's heart.

Herod, however, turns his heart toward himself and continues the curse of the generations. Paranoid that others would overthrow his power, Herod had already ordered the executions of several family members and close associates. Now, in an effort to kill the baby Jesus, the "king of the Jews," Herod demands the slaughter of every male child under age two.

Herod Antipas governs 4 B.C. to A.D. 39 after his father's death. Herod Antipas shares in the family curse, but God pursues him. Although Herod Antipas gave in to his wife's pressure to imprison John the Baptist, Mark 6:20 tells us, "Herod feared John and protected him, knowing him to be a righteous and holy man. When Herod heard John, he was greatly puzzled; yet he liked to listen to him."

Herod Antipas' heart is opening to God's Word. He enjoys listening to God's messenger. But one too many drinks at his own birthday party pushes Antipas to make a deadly mistake. Drunkenly enamored by his niece's dance, Herod Antipas vows to give her anything she desires up to half of his kingdom. She asks for John the Baptist's head. Corrupted by the women in his life, Antipas fails to break the generational curse.

Yet God continues to pursue Herod and gives him another chance (Luke 23:8-11). This time God steps in Himself when Jesus is put on trial in Herod's court. When Jesus gives no response to Herod's pointed questions, Herod joins his soldiers in vehemently ridiculing Jesus. Herod sends Jesus back to Pilate, and Luke 23:12 says, "That day Herod and Pilate became friends—before this they had been enemies." Herod sides with his enemy and falls short of seeing who God really is.

Herod Agrippa I, Antipas' nephew and a grandson of Herod the Great, takes over the throne for a short five years. Herod Agrippa persecutes the followers of Christ and executes James. Swayed by the cheers of the Jews, Herod also imprisons Peter (Acts 12:1-5). When an angel frees Peter, Herod Agrippa executes the guards. A short time later, Herod Agrippa accepts the praise of the people who call him their god, but God immediately strikes down this arrogant king and worms devour him. Another Herod dies consumed with self!

Herod Agrippa II continues in the steps of his father and father's father, and we see God once again bringing His light of truth to the Herod dynasty. The Apostle Paul is arrested, and because he is Roman, he eventually presents his case before Herod Agrippa. During his defense, Paul clearly explains the gospel of Christ to this Roman ruler.

Listening intently, Agrippa declares to Paul, "'You almost persuade me to become a Christian'" (Acts 26:28 NKJV). Notice Agrippa say *almost.* Generation after generation God seeks to draw close to the Herods, and they *almost* repent. The centuries-old generational curse is *almost* broken.

But shortly after hearing the Gospel, this self-absorbed Herod Agrippa moves to a farm at the base of Mount Vesuvius. The rest is history—Vesuvius erupts and buries the Herod family. The generations of Esau to the Herods are lost forever. In passing down a rich spiritual heritage, *almost* is not enough. *Almost* is the death of a generation.

indebted to idols

Unfortunately, wrong choices that lead to depravity of soul did not end with the Herods in ancient Italy. Psychologist and author Steve Arterburn, in *Surprised by God,* details the lives of the world's wealthiest and most powerful men in the early twentieth century. In 1923, nine of these elite moguls met in Chicago's Edgewater Beach Hotel with one consuming goal: corral the world's financial markets. Together these opulent capitalists nearly controlled the world by their fingertips.

Yet after this meeting of affluence and influence, each of these men traveled a bizarre and dismal course in history:

> Charles Schwab, a steel magnate, died bankrupt, having lived his last five years on borrowed money;
>
> Samuel Insel, president of the largest utility company in America, died penniless and a fugitive from justice;
>
> Howard Hopkins, president of the largest American gas company, went insane;
>
> Arthur Cotton, a great food speculator, died insolvent overseas;
>
> Richard Whitney, president of the New York Stock Exchange, served time in Sing Sing prison;
>
> Albert Fall, a cabinet member for the U.S. government, was pardoned from prison so he could die at home;
>
> Ibar Krueger, who headed up the world's largest land monopoly, committed suicide;
>
> Leon Fraiser, president of the International Settlement, committed suicide;
>
> Jesse Livermore, stock speculator, committed suicide.[3]

Not only did these once-wealthy men die poor, they died owned by their idols—idols that corrupted their joy, enslaved their souls, and escorted them to their death. You, too, have a choice of life or death that will affect future generations. What choice will you make?

You may not have sold your birthright, ridiculed Jesus to His face, or traded your soul for futures on the stock exchange, but you may be risking your family's future just the same. What idols have been passed down to you? What idols are you passing on to your children?

Idols are anything that distract you from fully following God and nurturing your family. A fast-paced schedule, television, computer games, the Internet, money, possessions, career, sports, relationships—all these seemingly harmless things can take your eyes off God and His best for your life.

Throughout Scripture God does not mince words when it comes to idols. In Leviticus 19:4 He warns, "Do not turn to idols," and in 1 John 5:21 He exhorts, "Dear children, keep yourselves from idols."

Idols possess insatiable appetites and they enslave us. The Apostle Paul writes, "'Everything is permissible for me'—but not everything is beneficial. 'Everything is permissible for me'—but I will not be mastered by anything" (1 Cor. 6:12). When your time and affections bow down to idols, the idols become your master.

Idols control with exponential power. An innocent activity can snowball into an all-consuming passion. Just look at King David. His glance at bathing Bathsheba led to adultery, conspiracy, murder, and political cover-up.

Idols devour us. What seems subtle at first can eventually smother us. Hosea 8:4 describes the destructive nature of idols: "They set up kings without my consent; they choose princes without my approval. With their silver and gold they make idols for themselves to their own destruction."

In time, we become our idols. Hosea 9:10b declares, "They consecrated themselves to that shameful idol and became as vile as the thing they loved." If you set your mind on the things of the flesh, you will reap the rewards of the flesh—hostility toward God and death (Rom. 8: 5-7). You are choosing life or death for your children. What choice will you make?

idols ensnare our children

Idols may elicit pleasure at the moment, but Hosea 8:7 says, "They sow the wind and reap the whirlwind." Idols leave us parched by the blistering winds of unfilled desire. Even if we pursue our idols in secret, they still affect those we love. How do idols affect our children? Our children will take from our homes what we live out in our homes.

Children hide our idols. Children are quick to pick up on our habits. They will literally protect the idols they see us pursue. We see this in Genesis 31:19 when Rachel hid her father's household idols.

Children remember our idols. We may forsake our idols, but they are not quickly forgotten in our children's minds. Jeremiah 17:2 speaks to this: "Even their children remember their altars and Asherah poles beside the spreading trees and on the high hills."

Children worship our idols. If we grow attached to and serve idols, our children will model our behavior. We read of this in King Amon's life. He grew up to be just like Daddy. "He walked in all the ways of his father; he worshiped the idols his father had worshiped, and bowed down to them. He forsook the LORD, the God of his fathers, and did not walk in the way of the LORD" (2 Kings 21:21-22).

The tragic result of allowing idols to edge their way into our lives and into our homes is that God will eventually turn His eyes away from our children and us: "Because you have ignored the law of your God, I also will ignore your children" (Hosea 4:6b).

Fortunately, we do not have to repeat the mistakes of the Herods and settle for *almost*. We can examine the attitudes and activities that we've let come between God and us and between our family and us. We can turn any idols over to our forgiving Father right now, and as He promises in 1 John 1:9, He will "forgive us our sins and purify us from all unrighteousness."

Once we've made a decision to abandon our idols, we, like the children of Israel, may be tempted to return to our idols. That's a painful mistake God's people made over and over throughout history. The Bible records in 2 Kings 17:33, "They worshiped the LORD, but they also served their own gods." God does not want us to *almost* serve Him wholeheartedly. He wants our *utmost* devotion, not what's left over from serving our own gods. He wants us to move forward in confidence and freedom with His plan for our lives and families.

plowing ahead

Many of us do not even have a plan for dinner let alone a plan for our children and the generations after them. In the Hebrew, plan means "to engrave or plow." Like a farmer who looks straight ahead in the distance to plow straight rows in his fields, so must we "fix our eyes on Jesus, the author and perfecter of our faith" (Heb. 12:2). We must plow ahead with a plan to choose life that our children might live (Deut. 30:19).

Before the Seneca tribe in the Northeast United States would make changes that would affect their families, the elders would ask, "How will this affect the next seven generations?"[4] The Senecas knew their plans today affected the tomorrow of at least seven generations! What a contrast to the Herods and the early twentieth-century tycoons.

We wrote this book to help you plan for your children's today and their tomorrows. Tying your children's heartstrings to God's truth involves creating meaningful celebrations to help your children remember God in their everyday lives. Celebrating the wonders of God starts in slowing down to savor the *kairos* moments with our kids.

Our culture and the idols it fashions are trying to steal our children and force them to live *almost* for God. Seventeen-year-old Vanesa Vathanasombat of Whittier, California, says in a May 2000 *Newsweek* report on American teens: "You are who you hang around with. Before, parents made you who you are. Now, teens are pretty much defined by their friends. I see my mom maybe an hour a day and not at all on weekends."

In the same article, seventeen-year-old Robertino Rodriguez gives his view on today's youth. "There's a lot of anger in my generation. You can hear it in the music. Kids are angry for a lot of reasons, but mostly because parents aren't around."[5]

This commentary on America's adolescents depicts the somber truth—the current generation is the most abandoned generation of young people in recent history. But you and I are changing that! And we are starting with our own families.

hiding our children

When God is about to do something great in history, He takes extraordinary care in hiding the children. Moses' parents hid him by faith for three months in their home and then hid him in a waterproof papyrus basket along the Nile (Ex. 2:1-3). Hannah gave up her only son so the priest Eli could hide Samuel in the temple and teach him to minister before the Lord (1 Sam. 1:24–2:11).

When evil Queen Mother Athaliah tried to destroy the entire royal family, God hid young Joash with his nurse in the temple of the Lord for six years before appointing him king of Judah at age seven (2 Kings 11:1-3). John the Baptist hid in the desert until his public ministry (Luke 1:80), and Mary and Joseph hid Jesus in Egypt (Matt. 2:13-14).

As parents, we are responsible for hiding our children from the schemes of the Enemy. How are you hiding your children? Your mantle as a parent is to guard, cover, and protect your children. You are to hide your children under the gifts of perspective, purpose, and protection.

"As Arthur Wing Pinero has written, 'The future is only the past again, entered through another gate.' Increasingly, Americans are sensing that the next great gate in history is approaching. It's time to trust our instincts, think seasonally, and *prepare*."[6]

How are you preparing to enter the next great gate of history? How are you preparing your children to step into the future? Setting up your own *Celebrations of Faith* is a crucial way to prepare.

Page back through this book and choose one celebration you can begin this week. Just choose one and watch God work in your family. Think through one way you can cherish some *kairos* moments with your kids today.

As speaker and author Tim Kimmel writes, "My job as a parent is a temporary responsibility with eternal consequences. The amount of time that my wife and I have to adequately develop a sense of inner security and personal adequacy within our children is fleeting. Incredibly brief."[7]

Your time to create an enduring legacy with your children is brief. Make the most of it! Isaiah 8:18 says, "Here am I, and the children the LORD has given me. We are signs and symbols in Israel from the LORD Almighty, who dwells on Mount Zion." You and your children are the signs and symbols of the Lord God Almighty in our culture. Are you willing to let Him display His glory through you?

Mothers, stand steadfast in faith even in the desert places. Cherish the godly women in your life who can help you weave a legacy of everlasting beauty. Fathers, fight as God's warriors to safeguard and bless your children. Remind your family that you are sturdy oaks of righteousness. In your family, choose words of life and celebrate God's truth.

A touching example of resolute parenting is the story of a flock of snow geese that laid their eggs and settled on their nests. As a fierce blizzard piled snow around their chilled bodies, the snow geese refused to abandon their eggs even for a breath of air. The geese were later found with their frozen necks stretched upward as they gasped for their last breaths. They suffocated holding fast to their commitment to their offspring and to each other.[8] *Are you willing to let nothing move you from your commitment to your children?*

God will give you all the wisdom, grace, and strength you need to stand committed to your children, even in the storms of life. "And God is able to make all grace abound to you, so that in all things at all times, having all that you need, you will abound in every good work" (2 Cor. 9:8).

The last words of the Old Testament, written about 450 years before Christ came to earth, promised a prophet who would "turn the hearts of the fathers to their children, and the hearts of the children to their fathers" (Mal. 4:6). God is still calling today for parents and children to turn their hearts toward each other.

No matter your past failings, your current circumstances, or your future unknowns—you can with God's unstoppable power—choose life over death and forsake all idols. "Now choose life, so that you and your children may live" (Deut. 30:19).

For God's sake, for your sake, for the sake of your numberless descendants yet to be born—you can create *Celebrations of Faith* that will turn the hearts of your children to follow Jehovah. You can move past *almost* and let God work His *utmost* in your life.

personal reflection

❀ What plan do I have to repent and turn from my idols?
❀ Who will I be accountable to in turning away from idols?
❀ In what areas of my life do I settle for *almost*?
❀ What are two or three things that I remember most about this book?
❀ How can I be immovable in my commitment to my children?

personal prayer

Lord God, Creator and Sustainer, the Beginning and the End of all things, I bow down before You asking You to create in me Your heart for my children. Sustain me in my weary, ordinary days when You are doing great things and I cannot see Your greatness. Begin in me new paths of purpose and plans to engrave Your deep truths into my children's memories. Hold me together in the palm of Your hand that I may finish well the course set before me and finish with joy.

Take any idols hidden in dark places in my heart and in my home, and cleanse me from all unrighteousness and fill me with Your holiness. Give me fresh vision in the small graces and small places of my home—a home that harbors Your very life and love to a fallen world. Take our moments and celebrations of Your glory and may they be magnified forever and ever . . . for a thousand generations to come!

Endnotes

Chapter One: *Our Children's Heartbeats*

1. Stephen R. Covey, *The Seven Habits of Highly Effective People* (New York: Simon & Schuster, 1989), 146.

2. Linda Dillow, *Calm My Anxious Heart* (Colorado Springs, Colo.: NavPress, 1998), 144.

3. Brenda Hunter, *Home by Choice* (Portland: Multnomah Press, 1991), 146-147.

4. Josh McDowell and Bob Hostetler, *Right From Wrong* (Dallas: Word Publishing, 1994), 47-48.

5. Dillow, *Calm My Anxious Heart,* 3.

6. James R. Lucas, *Proactive Parenting* (Eugene, Ore.: Harvest House, 1993), 53.

7. William R. Mattox Jr., "Why TR Loved Adventure, His Family and a Good Pillow Fight," *USA Today,* 17 June 1999, sec. A, p. 15.

Chapter Two: *A Mother's Legacy*

1. Susan Chira, *A Mother's Place* (New York: HarperCollins Publishers, 1998), 26.

2. Iris Krasnow, *Surrendering to Motherhood* (New York: Hyperion, 1997), 207.

3. William Strauss and Neil Howe, *Generations: The History of America's Future 1584 to 2069* (New York: William Morrow and Company, 1991), 64.

4. John A. Stormer, *Growing Up God's Way* (Florissant, Mo.: Liberty Bell Press, 1984), 43.

5. Strauss and Howe, *Generations,* 168.

6. Catherine Marshall, *Something More* (New York: Avon Books, 1974), 67.

7. MOPS International, *A Mother's Touch,* (Grand Rapids, Mich.: Zondervan Publishing, 1998), 90.

Chapter Three: *The Father Warrior*

1. Stephen R. Covey, A. Roger Merrill, and Rebecca R. Merrill, *First Things First* (New York: Simon & Schuster, 1994), 32.

2. *The Student Bible, New International Version* (Grand Rapids, Mich.: Zondervan Publishing, 1996), 1114.

3. Robert Hicks, *The Masculine Journey,* (Colorado Springs, Colo.: NavPress, 1993), 71-88.

4. Peter Bizkind, "He Stars, She Stars," *Vanity Fair* , February 2000, 117.

5. Robert Sullivan, "Dad Again," *LIFE* , June 1999, 68.

6. Oswald Chambers, *My Utmost for His Highest* (Uhrichsville, Ohio: Barbour

and Company, 1963),189.

7. Ken R. Canfield, *The 7 Secrets of Effective Fathers* (Wheaton, Ill.: Tyndale House Publishers, 1992), 42.

8. Richard A. Swenson, M.D., *Margin* (Colorado Springs, Colo.: NavPress, 1992), 154.

9. Stu Weber, *Tender Warrior* (Sisters, Ore.:Multnomah, 1993), 25.

10. Richard A. Swenson, M.D., *The Overload Syndrome* (Colorado Springs, Colo.: NavPress, 1998), 178.

11. Donald T. Phillips, *Lincoln on Leadership* (New York: Warner Books, 1992), 113.

12. Theodore Roosevelt, *History as Literature, Part IV:* "Citizenship in a Republic," part of the *Selected Works of Theodore Roosevelt, Vol. VI* (New York: Charles Scribner's Sons, 1913).

13. Dr. Larry Crabb Jr. and Lawrence Crabb Sr., *God of My Father* (Grand Rapids, Mich.: Zondervan Publishing, 1994), 9.

Chapter Four: *The Grace of Remembering*

1. *God's Little Instruction Book for Mom* (Tulsa, Okla.: Honor Books, 1994).

Chapter Five: *The Joshua Basket*

1. Swenson, *The Overload Syndrome,* 93.

Chapter Eight: *The Scripture Recital*

1. Brenda Hunter, Ph.D., *The Power of Mother Love* (Colorado Springs, Colo.: Waterbrook Press, 1997), 210.

2. John Angell James, *Female Piety* (Morgan, Penn.: Soli Deo Gloria Publications, 1995), 340.

Chapter Ten: *Personal Beliefs Statement*

1. John Bevere, *Breaking Intimidation* (Lake Mary, Fla.: Creation House, 1995), 176.

2. Neil T. Anderson, *The Bondage Breaker*, (Eugene, Ore.: Harvest House, 1993), 193-195. Used by permission.

Chapter Twelve: *Mom and Dad's Book of Treasures*

1. Sarah Ban Breathnach, "Three Steps to the Simply Abundant Life," *Family Circle*, May 9, 2000, 36.

Chapter Thirteen: *Celebrate the Sabbath*

1. James, *Female Piety*, 335.

Chapter Fourteen: *The Secret Place*

1. Lester Sumrall, *The Names of God* (Springdale, Penn.: Whitaker House, 1993), 47.

2. Mary Pipher, Ph.D., *The Shelter of Each Other* (New York: Grossman/Putnam, 1996), 234.

Chapter Fifteen: *Who Am I?*

1. Bob Greene and Oprah Winfrey, *Make the Connection* (New York: Hyperion, 1996), 4.

2. Noah Webster, *First Edition of an American Dictionary of the English Language* (San Francisco: Foundation for American Christian Education, 1995).

3. Anderson, *The Bondage Breaker,* 213-214. Used by permission.

Chapter Sixteen: *Oaks of Righteousness*

1. Rhoda Thomas Tripp, *The International Thesaurus of Quotations* (New York: Harper & Row, 1970), 601.

2. Tripp, *The International Thesaurus of Quotations*, 713.

3. Merrill F. Unger, *Unger's Bible Dictionary* (Chicago: Moody Press, 1980), 800.

Chapter Seventeen: *Celebrate the Home*

1. Mary Farrar, *Choices* (Sisters, Ore.: Multnomah, 1994), 69, 71.

2. Swenson, *The Overload Syndrome*, 155.

3. Peter Johnson, "TV Grabs Biggest Share of Kids' Time," *USA Today*, 18 November 1999.

4. Michael Medved and Diane Medved, Ph.D., *Saving Childhood* (New York: HarperCollins, 1998), 19.

5. Dottie Enrico, "Connecting Mothers Online," *USA Today*, 17 November 1999.

Chapter Eighteen: *Character Trophy*

1. Neil T. Anderson, *Victory Over the Darkness* (Ventura, Calif.: Regal Books, 1990), 43.

Chapter Nineteen: *Wisdom Teas*

1. Webster, *First Edition of an American Dictionary of the English Language*.

2. Shmuley Boteach, *Kosher Sex* (New York: Main Street Books, Doubleday, 1999), 256.

Chapter Twenty: *Legacy Tea*
1. James, *Female Piety*, 330.

Chapter Twenty-Three: *Celebration of Manhood*
1. Weber, *Tender Warrior*, 139.
2. Bill and Nancie Carmichael, *The Best Things Ever Said About Parenting* (Wheaton, Ill.: Tyndale House Publishers, 1996), 192.
3. Michael Gurian, *The Wonder of Boys* (New York: Penguin Putnam, 1996), 153.
4. Hicks, *The Masculine Journey*, 85.
5. Gurian, *The Wonder of Boys*, 126.

Chapter Twenty-Four: *Hearts and Habits of Heroes*
1. Michael Gurian, *A Fine Young Man* (New York: Penguin Putnam, 1998), 6.
2. Ibid., 66.
3. Ibid., 64.
4. Gurian, *The Wonder of Boys*, 149.
5. William Beausay II, *Boys!* (Nashville: Thomas Nelson, 1994), 137.
6. Ibid., 193.
7. Ibid., 19.

Chapter Twenty-Five: *Family Foundations*
1. *God's Little Instruction Book for Mom.*
2. Webster, *Noah Webster's First Edition of An American Dictionary of the English Language.*
3. Tim Kimmel, *Little House on the Freeway* (Portland: Multnomah Press, 1987), 180-181.

Chapter Twenty-Six: *The Blessing Ceremony*
1. Gary Smalley and John Trent, Ph.D., *The Blessing* (Nashville: Thomas Nelson, 1986).

Chapter Twenty-Seven: *The Blessing Journal*
1. *God's Little Instruction Book for Mom.*

Chapter Twenty-Eight: *Celebrate Truth*
1. Pipher, *The Shelter of Each Other*, 267.
2. Francis P. Martin, *Hung by the Tongue* (Lafayette, La.: Francis P. Martin, 1979), 18.
3. Josh McDowell, speech at Focus on the Family Physician's Conference, October 1999, Colorado Springs, Colo.

Chapter Twenty-Nine: *Words of Life*
1. Jaya Chaliha and Edward Le Joly, comps. *The Joy of Living* (New York: Viking Penguin, 1997), 80.
2. Shad Helmstetter, *Choices* (New York: Simon & Schuster, 1989), 149.
3. *God's Little Instruction Book for Mom.*
4. Covey, *The Seven Habits of Highly Effective People*, 46.
5. Tim Kimmel, *Raising Kids Who Turn Out Right* (Sisters, Ore.: Multnomah Books, 1993), 87, 91.
6. Florence Littauer, *Silver Boxes* (Dallas: Word Publishing, 1989), 147.

Chapter Thirty: *Family Covenant*
1. Daniel A. Brown, Ph.D., *Unlock the Power of Family* (Nashville: Sparrow Press, 1994), 114.

Chapter Thirty-One: *Choose Life!*
1. James R. Lucas, *Proactive Parenting* (Eugene, Ore.: Harvest House, 1993), 155.
2. Marilyn Hickey, *Break the Generation Curse* (Denver: Marilyn Hickey Ministries, 1988), 51-57.
3. Stephen Arterburn, *Surprised by God* (Colorado Springs, Colo.: Focus on the Family Publishing, 1997), 13.
4. Pipher, *The Shelter of Each Other*, 89.
5. Sharon Begley, "A World of Their Own," *Newsweek*, 8 May 2000.
6. William Strauss and Neil Howe, *The Fourth Turning* (New York: Broadway Books, 1997), 22.
7. Kimmel, *Little House on the Freeway*, 168.
8. Louis Gordon, Carol Gordon, and Kathryn Butler Turner, *The Child Heart* (Bethany, Okla.: Heart Menders, Inc., 1990), 17.

Resources

Fatherhood:

Beausay, William. *Boys!* Nashville: Thomas Nelson, 1994.

Blankenhorn, David. *Fatherless America*. New York: Basic Books, 1995.

Bryan, Mark. *Prodigal Fathers*. New York: Clarkson Potter, 1997.

Canfield, Ken R. *The 7 Secrets of Effective Fathers*. Wheaton, Ill.: Tyndale House Publishers, 1992.

Crabb, Dr. Larry Jr. and Lawrence Crabb Sr. *God of My Father*. Grand Rapids, Mich.: Zondervan Publishing, 1994.

Gilder, George. *Men and Marriage*. Gretna: Pelican Publishing Co., 1986.

Gurian, Michael. *A Fine Young Man*. New York: Penguin Putnam, 1998.

Gurian, Michael. *The Wonder of Boys*. New York: Penguin Putnam, 1996.

Hicks, Robert. *The Masculine Journey*. Colorado Springs, Colo.: NavPress, 1993.

Lewis, Paul. *The Five Key Habits of Smart Dads*. Grand Rapids, Mich.: Zondervan Publishing, 1994.

Lewis, Robert. *Raising a Modern Day Knight*. Colorado Springs, Colo.: Focus on the Family, 1999.

Park, Ross D and Armin A. Brott. *Throwaway Dads*. Boston: Houghton Mifflin, 1999.

Vitz, Paul C. *Faith of the Fatherless*. Dallas: Spence Publishing, 2000.

Weber, Stu. *Tender Warrior*. Sisters, Ore.: Multnomah, 1993.

Motherhood:

Farrar, Mary. *Choices*. Sisters, Ore.: Multnomah Books, 1994.

Fleming, Anne T. *Motherhood Deferred*. Columbine, NY: Fawcette, 1994. *

George, Elizabeth. *A Woman After God's Heart*. Eugene, Ore.: Harvest House, 1997.

God's Little Instruction Book for Mom. Tulsa, Okla.: Honor Books, 1994.

Graglia, F. Carolyn. *Domestic Tranquility*. Dallas: Spence Publishing, 1998.*

Hunter, Brenda. *Home by Choice*. Portland: Multnomah Press, 1991.

Hunter, Brenda, Ph.D. *The Power of Mother Love*. Colorado Springs, Colo.: Waterbrook Press, 1997.

James, John Angell. *Female Piety*. Morgan, Penn.: Soli Deo Gloria Publications, 1995.

Krasnow, Iris. *Surrendering to Motherhood*. New York: Hyperion, 1997.*

Pipher, Mary, Ph.D. *The Shelter of Each Other*. New York: Grossman/Putnam, 1996.

* Contain strong feminist language—read with discretion.

Parenting:

Backus, William and Candice Backus. *Teaching Your Children to Tell Themselves the Truth*. Minneapois, Minn.: Bethany House, 1992.

Brown, Daniel A., Ph.D. *Unlock the Power of Family*. Nashville: Sparrow Press, 1994.

Carmichael, William and Nancie. *The Best Things Ever Said About Parenting* Wheaton, Ill.: Tyndale House, 1996.

Carmichael, William and Nancie Carmichael. *Lord, Bless My Child*. Wheaton, Ill.: Tyndale House, 1995.

Dobson, James C. *Solid Answers*. Wheaton, Ill.: Tyndale House, 1997.

Fugate, Richard. *What the Bible Says About Child Training*. Tempe, Ariz.: Alethia Division of Alpha Omega Publishing, 1980.

Glaspey, Terry W. *Children of a Greater God*. Out of print.

Gordon, Louis, Carol Gordon, and Kathryn Butler Turner. *The Child Heart*. Bethany, Okla.: Heart Mender, Inc., 1990.

Kimmel, Tim. *Little House on the Freeway*. Portland, Ore.: Multnomah Press, 1987.

Kimmel, Tim. *Raising Kids Who Turn Out Right*. Sisters, Ore.: Multnomah Books, 1993.

Linamen, Karen Scalf. *The Parent Warrior*. Grand Rapids, Mich.: Fleming Revell, 1999.

Lucas, James R. *Proactive Parenting*. Eugene, Ore.: Harvest House, 1993.

McDowell, Josh and Bob Hostetler. *Right From Wrong*. Dallas: Word Publishing, 1994.

Medved, Michael and Diane Medved, Ph.D. *Saving Childhood*. New York: HarperCollins, 1998.

Murray, *How to Raise Your Child for Christ*. Out of print.

Rainey, Dennis. *One Home at a Time*. Wheaton, Ill.: Tyndale House, 1999.

Stormer, John A. *Growing Up God's Way*. Florissant, Mo.: Liberty Bell Press, 1984.

Strauss, William and Neil Howe. *Generations: A History of America's Future*. New York: William Morrow and Company, 1991.

Swenson, Richard A., M.D. *Margin*. Colorado Springs, Colo.: NavPress, 1992.

Wilson, Randy and Lisa. *Daddy's Blessing*. Colorado Springs, Colo.: Cook Communications, 2001.

Wilson, Randy and Lisa. *The Joshua Basket*. Colorado Springs, Colo.: Cook Communications, 2001.

Yates, John and Susan Yates. *What Really Matters at Home*. Dallas: Word Publishing, 1992.

Resources

Leadership:

Covey, Stephen R., A. Roger Merrill, and Rebecca R. Merrill. *First Things First*. New York: Simon & Schuster, 1994.

Covey, Stephen R. *The Seven Habits of Highly Effective People*. New York: Simon & Schuster, 1989.

Mouser, William, *Five Aspects of Man* (Bible study course). Out of print.

Mouser, Barbara K., *Five Aspects of Woman* (Bible study course), Waxahachie, Tex.: International Council for Gender Studies, 1995.

Phillips, Donald T. *Lincoln on Leadership*. New York: Warner Books, 1992.

Stanley, Paul D. and J. Robert Clinton. *Connecting*. Colorado Springs, Colo.: NavPress, 1992.

Swenson, Richard A., M.D. *The Overload Syndrome*. Colorado Springs, Colo.: NavPress, 1998.

Thrall, Bill, Bruce McNicol, and Ken McElrath. *The Ascent of a Leader*. San Francisco: Jossey-Bass Publishers, 1999.

Warren, Rick. *Purpose Driven Life* (Bible Study). Grand Rapids, Mich.: Zondervan Publishing, 2000.

Devotional/Personal Growth:

Anderson, Neil T. *The Bondage Breaker*. Eugene, Ore.: Harvest House, 1993.

Anderson, Neil T. *Victory Over the Darkness*. Ventura, Calif.: Regal Books, 1990.

Arterburn, Stephen. *Surprised by God*. Colorado Springs, Colo.: Focus on the Family, 1997.

Bevere, John. *Breaking Intimidation*. Lake Mary, Fla.: Creation House, 1995.

Blackaby, Henry. *Experiencing God* (Bible study). Nashville: Broadman & Holman Publishing, 1993.

Chambers, Oswald. *My Utmost for His Highest*. Uhrichsville, Ohio: Barbour and Company, 1963.

Dillow, Linda. *Calm My Anxious Heart*. Colorado Springs, Colo.: NavPress, 1998.

Garborg, Rolf. *Family Blessing*. Dallas: Word Publishing, 1994.

Hickey, Marilyn. *Break the Generation Curse*. Denver: Marilyn Hickey Ministries, 1988.

Littauer, Florence. *Silver Boxes*. Dallas: Word Publishing, 1989.

Marshall, Catherine. *Something More*. New York: McGraw-Hill, 1974.

Smalley, Gary and John Trent, Ph.D. *The Blessing*. Nashville: Thomas Nelson, 1986.

Sumrall, Lester. *The Names of God*. Springdale, Penn.: Whitaker House, 1993.

Townsend, Dr. John. *Hiding From Love*. Colorado Springs, Colo.: NavPress, 1991.

A Personal Note From the **Author**

Heart

Living in the moments with our children takes an enormous amount of emotional and spiritual energy and planning! We, like you, juggle children, ballet, ice hockey, school, ministry, and work, and there are days when we are just flat-out exhausted. We also fight to maintain the "moments" in this culture of instant-messages and e-mails. The only way to tie our children's hearts to the truth is to just do it! God is not impressed with our to-do lists, but with our values, as we seek Him daily.

Soul

The Scripture passage that most fervently conveys our hearts is Psalm 78:5-7. We pray this will be your passion as well.
"He commanded our forefathers to teach their children, so the next generation would know them, even the children yet to be born, and they in turn would tell their children. Then they would put their trust in God and would not forget his deeds, but would keep his commands."

Mind

We pray He will guide you continually as you seek His face in teaching your children His ways. For further study, we recommend the resources listed in the book. These, in particular, will be helpful: *Raising Children Right*, by Tim Kimmel; *Lord Bless My Child*, by Bill and Nancie Carmichael; *Right from Wrong*, by Josh McDowell; and our *The Joshua Basket* and *Daddy's Blessing* packages.

Strength

Fractured families can only be healed at the feet of Jesus. Our desire is that *Celebrations of Faith* will not complicate your life, but simplify it. Ponder these suggestions as you begin to incorporate celebrations in your family.

Rituals create significance. Choose carefully a celebration that best suits the needs and ages of your children and will be the most meaningful to them.

Begin with just one celebration and make it yours. Be consistent, place it on your calendar, and ask God to bless it.

Don't be afraid of failure! If one celebration doesn't fit, don't force it. Just try another one!

You may want to commit to meet with another family monthly to do a celebration and keep each other accountable. This is a lot of fun.

We pray that God will bless you as you exalt Him with your children! His pleasure rests on you. On your worst days, you are His delight! No one else can parent those children like you. He is cheering you on from the heavens—for your legacy to mark generations to come!

Standing with you on holy ground,